AMERICA BETWEEN THE EXTREMISTS

"We are never deceived.
We deceive ourselves."

GOETHE

AMERICA BETWEEN
THE EXTREMISTS

A NEW APPROACH
TO POLITICAL MATURITY

by

DOUGLAS BOGGS

EXPOSITION PRESS   **NEW YORK**

EXPOSITION PRESS INC.

50 Jericho Turnpike   Jericho, New York 11753

FIRST EDITION

LIBRARY OF CONGRESS CATALOG CARD NUMBER: 68-8000

EP 46866

TO THE IDEAS AND MEMORY

OF

EDMUND BURKE

Prologue

The main part of this book was written in the summer of 1967, the Introduction in November of that year and this Prologue and the author's note that appears on pp. 73–76, in July, 1968. The Introduction is an attempt to present the moderate position in American politics as a hip, dynamic doctrine and to protest the suggestion that the middle-of-the-roader is, by definition, indecisive. In fact it will be argued that the American moderate represents the true conservative and defender of the American Revolution and that that revolution, in spite of those members of the New Left who may protest, is the very essence of hip. I will use the admitted gimmick of a sketchy historical narrative, commenting freely and drawing parallels with the contemporary American political scene as we progress.

In a way, the Introduction might have been an Epilogue, for it is an assessment of our situation in November, 1967. At that time we appeared to be headed into a depression of major proportions. A big money sell-off at the top began on the New York Stock Exchange in 1965, shortly after the Vietnam War was accelerated. (See pp. 77–87.) Since then two major events have made the monetary picture slightly brighter: (1) President Johnson's speech of March 31, 1968, in which he announced he would not run again and would try to negotiate a peace in Vietnam, signaled a tremendous rally on the New York Stock Exchange.

The President's speech came just when we appeared to be about two weeks away from a major panic, and it is a good guess that this, and perhaps pressure by central bankers at the Stockholm meeting in March when the current plan to set up "paper gold" was launched, may have had much to do with the timing of the announcement. (2) A massive loan for the faltering British pound was announced on July 8, 1968, and this also came at a very late date. (See pp. 74, 75.)

We are, in fact, far from out of the storm, but we do have some breathing time in which to put our house in order. Whether the Vietnam War is ended in the near future or not, we felt that the greatest service to readers would be not to revise the Introduction and analysis of the financial panic, but rather to leave them essentially as they were written in 1967 in order to illustrate the folly of that war.

Since writing this book last summer, the assassinations of Martin Luther King and Senator Robert Kennedy have served to underscore and strengthen the arguments advanced throughout. The abortive chaos in France, the earlier than expected hardening of the New Left, and the spate of senseless, everyday murders going on at the present time are all further evidence of our shaky foundations.

This book pulls no punches. It jabs hard at the Right *and* the Left, the middle-aged, middle-class authority *and* the hippies. As such it is bound to create controversy, and indeed that is the intention. No one will agree with all of the ideas herein. Many will not agree with most of them. While liberally interspersed with lesser ideas and theories, probably the most important arguments are: (1) That totalitarianism is an outgrowth of romanticism, and while the former is in opposition to democracy, the latter is a reaction to the Enlightenment upon which Western democracy is based. (2) That totalitarianism began to creep into the Western democracies during World War I when the total effort of society was directed toward defeating the enemy. At present the tide seems to be turning in favor of the final victory of totalitarianism over democracy (particularly if we encounter a depression). The current rash of violence in the United States is one of the primary danger signals. (3) That the Far Right in this country, whose philosophical roots can be traced more to romanticism than to the Enlightenment, represents the counterrevolution to the American Revolution just as much as does the radical Left.

Preface

Any author, particularly of non-fiction, finds himself indebted to so many people that it is not only impractical to thank them all publicly but impossible to remember everyone. I am especially indebted to the hundreds of friends and acquaintances who have stimulated many of the thoughts found in the text. Where occasionally an idea is clearly someone else's, it has been noted as such. Usually, however, an idea becomes changed until it is an author's own to the extent that it seems pointless to bore the reader with such detail. I would also like to thank all of my teachers, especially Dr. Leo F. Solt, chairman of the Indiana University Department of History, who is directly responsible for planting the seed which inspired this work. Publishers have been most cooperative and helpful in giving me permission to quote or to reproduce statistical data; they are noted in the text. I am also grateful to Mrs. Clemence Chase for helping with proof-reading and criticism. Above all this work owes its existence to two young women—to my sister, Leah B. Boggs, for her tremendous secretarial help over and above her more than full-time job, and to Kay, who provided the domestic atmosphere which enabled me to start this project.

D. B.

CONTENTS

"No nation acquires the power of judgment unless it can pass judgment upon itself. But to this great privilege it can only attain at a very late stage."

—GOETHE

Introduction

As this manuscript heads for the publisher, the Vietnam crisis is becoming clearer in all its alarming aspects. The financial panic, the threat of extremists' taking power in the nuclear-armed United States, and the demoralization of the American people to an extent not seen in over a century are all ramifications of the Vietnam War. But in a broader sense, the Great Vietnam Crisis and its accompanying problems are a result of the cold war and the official policies of our government since 1949. The overreaction to the highanded actions of Stalin nearly fifteen years after his death seems about to bury us, just as Stalin's successor predicted. If this crisis continues to its awful, logical conclusion, Ho Chi Minh, who has acted as if he has had the world's foremost monetary authority at his disposal since the war began in earnest in 1965, may go down as the man of the century. For the stakes in this crisis are no less than Western civilization itself. The United States, whose administration and people in the main have not yet been able to muster enough humility to admit the error that has been committed, is nearing a monetary crisis which may menace the solvency of the United States government as well as her allies. Forty years ago individuals were bankrupt. Today, when it is behind the banks, farmers, veterans, and home-owners, to name a few, the United States government has clearly risked its very existence on the cold-war prosperity and the ability to avoid a full-blown money panic. This time, barring a repudiation of the national debt, the United States may be headed not only for a depression but also for a runaway inflation of the kind experienced in Germany in the 1920's. If this comes, it will be plainly evident to all that we are impotent in Vietnam.

The problems, unfortunately, are still more complicated than this. What effect a depression might have upon an astounded American people cannot be determined in advance. But some of the strains running through the anguish of a moralistic, arrogant people faced with their first military defeat, however distant from their shores, and faced with chaos at home as a result of that defeat, are plainly evident. Drop-the-bombers are on the rise. The New Left has adopted the totalitarian-tinged tactics displayed by the Young Republicans at the 1964 Republican Convention when Governors Rockefeller and Romney were shouted down. And the Left is being criticized much more widely than the Right at this time. The real possibility of a bloodbath in this country is looming. Reactionaries with the gall to call themselves conservatives are showing alarming signs of hardening into true fascists in large numbers. The Negroes and the leftists are already marked by many of these people as the Jews were marked in pre-Nazi Germany.

All this would not seem to present such a clear and present danger if it were not for a developing world-wide monetary crisis. A major economic collapse should be the great equalizer, for even the wealthiest individual who is solely in cash, as well as the short seller, could not hide from real runaway inflation. The possible effects of this dilemma are many and varied. If a drop-the-bomber were to assume the presidency, with the Soviet Union committed to retaliation, then the Vietnam War might have indeed been the start of World War III and annihilation for both East and West. Americans must not take the world down with them in a fit of egocentricity. Even if the United States withdraws without an act of genocide, we must guard against a myth similar to the "stab in the back" that arose in Germany after World War I because the Germans were not told the truth about their reverses during the war. Such a myth could bring us fascism several years from this writing. Moreover, if we tested the nuclear credibility of the Soviet Union with regard to Vietnam and found that the Soviets were not willing to cease to exist in this crisis, and therefore did not retaliate directly against us, it seems more than likely that in the United States itself the annihilation of Hanoi (or other populated North Vietnamese area) would be taken as an immediate signal for a full-scale internal bloodbath bordering on at least a small civil war. (Although the very reason this book was conceived was to appeal for moderation, an imminent threat of nuclear war initiated by the United States would have to be stopped at all costs. No true patriot could stand aside and approve such an act, particularly if it were an arrogant defense of our own official mistakes.)

If full-scale civil war broke out in this nation as a result of the complex Vietnam mess, the uncompromising camps that the United States people would find themselves having to choose between seem rather clear. On the one hand would be a hard-core fascist nucleus with decent organization, and on the other would be a mishmash of Black Nationalists, a few Reds (who are gradually increasing in number as a result of the administration's refusal to reason about the war and who may proliferate once the Far Right begins to persecute them and hunger begins to hit the nation), New Leftists, moderate socialists, and moderate conservatives who may grasp at such an impossible straw in an attempt to conserve the American Revolution and democracy. The latter conglomeration of anti-fascists would probably have no more organization than the losing side in the Spanish Civil War. Even if they were to win the war against the fascists, the fight for dominance amongst themselves would probably be ready to begin—as we have seen in the massacres of both the French and Russian revolutions in which the Liberal majorities (in the classical sense of the word *Liberal*) initiated the revolts but made no specific statement of goals and let the revolution get out of control by taking no precautionary steps designed to insure control in the early stages.

These dark prospects are not predictions. They are only possibilities that every moderate American of either liberal or conservative economic stripe must guard against with all urgency.

The great dream of the men who founded this nation is in serious jeopardy as the United States nears its two hundredth birthday. If the moderates—the true conservatives who would conserve the American Revolution—are to emerge from this crisis in control, that control must be solidified by a truly self-critical understanding of ourselves. We must understand exactly where our greatness lies as well as recognize our shortcomings and what our mistakes have been. If this understanding is realized by the mass of the American people, then those who have kept faith in the American idea will find that they have been vindicated. The Great Vietnam Crisis presents us with the first complete test of that greatness, for no people are great until they have proven their maturity by emerging from a great error with grace and humility. With the possible exception of economic collapse, all other dark possibilities may be avoided; and even if some of them do materialize, all is not lost. There are two, and only two, of the above contingencies which are likely to destroy the United States forever: (1) a dictatorship of either Right or Left, the Right being the more likely to emerge, in which freedom of speech and criticism of the government are thrown out the window for the foreseeable future, and (2) a nuclear genocide of the North Vietnamese people, which would possibly destroy much of the civilization of both East and West. (A bloodbath would of course make a dictatorship in America likely.) Even the financial situation might possibly be saved by a great gesture of humility by President Johnson toward a cease-fire before the collapse; a severe restraint on our spending and a steep and immediate rise in taxes, much higher than the 10 per cent that is being proposed; a release of the artificially pegged dollar to freely fluctuate until it finds its own proper if painful level in relation to gold and the world currencies; and a closing of the nation's stock exchanges by the boards of governors of the exchanges (for as long as three months if necessary) at the signal of competent technical analysts that a crash appears likely to begin the following day. (Such a precedent was established in 1914: in that year a stock-market panic was nipped in the bud when the New York Stock Exchange closed from July to December.)

Since there seems to be little likelihood in the present political climate that such efforts to save the economy of the Western nations will have been made in time, we seem to be faced with all the consequences of that unwise war at their worst. Our crass materialism, all too similar in nature to the materialism of Soviet socialism and National Socialism, made us so unwilling to sacrifice any of our prosperity that we may eventually lose it all. After fifteen to twenty years of the most fantastic prosperity the world had ever known, the Gallup poll indicated that 60 per cent of Americans still considered the family budget their most urgent problem in 1967.[1] Slums, which, contrary to popular opinion in this country, are virtually non-existent in most European nations, are still very much with us today. It would seem that if the pursuit of happiness is to be our criterion, the great cold-war boom has been in vain and our oft-lamented materialism has indeed proven shallow. I have even encountered in recent weeks a few otherwise rational and fairly well informed individuals who propose dropping the bomb rather than passing the 10 per cent surcharge—such economic reasoning being the only argument forwarded. Our task will be to inculcate a sincere acceptance of our responsibility (not guilt) for the present dilemma and consequently to develop a humility which we must have if we are to profit from our errors. But this education should come from the American people themselves instead of from the government, for that has failed us in the past, notably during the Johnson and Eisenhower administrations. (Nevertheless, as the German leaders of the Weimar Republic found out, we cannot afford to allow ultraconservatives and stab-in-the-backers to become dominant in our public schools. Loyalty oaths to the Constitution should be enforced with regard to the Right as well as the Left.)

If monetary chaos comes, Americans must work together. We may have to choose between a runaway inflation and, with all due respect to Alexander Hamilton, a tragic repudiation of the national debt. The latter act also brings with it the danger of a dictatorship to quell open rebellion. But other governments have

---

[1] *Time*, Nov. 10, 1967, p. 23.

gone through both runaway inflation and debt repudiation and survived. If we choose the runaway inflation, normal times will of course eventually return. We must not despair. If debt repudiation becomes the lesser of two evils, it could be done by a national referendum. It must not be done by a military dictatorship. Then any action necessary to enforce the desires of the people in order to begin rebuilding should be found constitutional. For although the Constitution gave Congress power to make laws, the legal doctrine of impossibility may be applicable here. The United States Constitution was not made to be discarded simply because the United States government mistakenly thought it was economically omnipotent for a generation. Humility should dominate our thinking here too. Our government can only perform the possible. Those who persist in expecting more, either in war or in domestic affairs, can only lead us to destruction.

As for the most horrifying possibility of all, nuclear war, even the ascension of a drop-the-bomber to the White House would not automatically mean that the bomb would indeed be dropped. Let the reader imagine for a moment that such a man is elected. This man, no matter what his former position in government, short of the cabinet and some of the military inner circle, would at first probably have too distant a view of diplomatic reality to allow him to make a decision. (Some military men who should know better, however, seem credible enough with regard to their capability of making such decisions.) While our drop-the-bomber was being introduced to his new office by the outgoing President and while he was feeling his way about in the first weeks, he would be faced with the stark reality of being eyeball to eyeball with hundreds of nuclear warheads. He would then probably realize rather suddenly that the fate of his beloved country and even of Western civilization very likely depended upon his restraint. This should be enough to cause any sane man to seek alternatives. Congress might also have the time and inclination to begin emergency legislation restraining the power of the President to strike the first nuclear blow and to try to limit the President's authority to initiate any military act without a decla-

ration of war except in *narrowly defined* and clear-cut incidents
of self-defense. Such a revision of the presidential powers in
keeping with the realities of the nuclear age could be a positive
result of the Vietnam tragedy.

The primary objection of many American citizens to unilateral
withdrawal from Vietnam[2] seems to be the fear that the other
Western democracies would cease to be committed to the defense
of their own cultures and modes of life. I do not think this fear
is well founded. On the contrary, it seems to be just another off-
shoot of our egocentric view of the world. Many of the Western
democracies, especially Great Britain and the English-speaking
parts of the Commonwealth in North America and Oceania, as
well as Scandinavia and the Benelux countries, are probably even
more committed to Western democratic institutions than we ourselves. But we have managed to frighten them with our apparent
immaturity as the leader of the Western world. Since the Vietnam
War became a major war, most of our allies have assumed a
rather horrified neutral position. Now that we have a chance to
prove our political maturity through a great act of humility, the
Western Alliance should be strengthened rather than weakened.
For such proper humility should only convince our natural allies
that here indeed is a worthy nation which has finally become a
seasoned asset, instead of being a contingent liability, to mutual
self-preservation. Such a change of attitude, if it actually emerged,
would provide a truer strengthening of the West from the inside
out than any limited war we could win (or any fantastic space
feat we could accomplish). Our allies would very likely rally
around us with enthusiasm for the first time since the pre-Dulles
days. President Johnson himself, at this writing, could still go
down in history as one of the greatest of all American Presidents,
as he has always wanted to be remembered, by admitting the
terrible blunder himself and ordering withdrawal. Such withdrawal would probably enable us to reach the more comfortable

---

[2] See the excellent moderate alternative to immediate and complete withdrawal proposed by John Kenneth Galbraith in "Resolving Our Vietnam
Predicament," *Playboy*, Dec., 1967, pp. 139 ff.

stage which should have always been the goal of our emergence from isolationism—that of a bona fide partner in European affairs rather than the callow boss of the whole show.

Finally, if our future is to have any meaning and if any lessons are to be learned from this unpleasant experience, we must accept two fundamental truths which the Vietnam crisis illustrates: (1) Democracy cannot long survive in this age in a nation that is armed to its nuclear teeth. The overriding goal of governments of both East and West must be bilateral nuclear disarmament with all possible speed. (2) Much less important but still highly treasured by most of us, provided it is reasonably regulated, is capitalism—*not to be confused with democracy.* If capitalism is to be preserved through the democratic process, or any process, then it must become poverty-oriented rather than prosperity (or materialistically) oriented.

We are faced with what is looking more and more like the great crisis toward which the events of the cold war have been pointing for the past twenty years. America is in fantastic need of great leaders to step forward, as they have so frequently for two centuries. Above all she is in need of both the humility and the forgivenesss of her people. It is to the hope that these needs will be met that this book is dedicated.

AMERICA BETWEEN THE EXTREMISTS

There are no bad peoples!
But without any pity
I am going to tell you
Without accusing the hosts
That each people has its wretched creatures.
I'll tell you about these skunks,
Listen to me!
I knew about fascism
                  through books
                       and movies,
And here I saw it in action.
Fascism stood up in my face smelling of whisky . . .
Fascism was noisily chewing gum.
It was sniveling
        covered with pimples
                    and
                tow-haired . . .
And if I had not been a Communist before,
That night
      I would have become a Communist.

EVGENY EVTUSHENKO

*after anti-Communist riots in Helsinki
during the World Youth Festival, summer of 1962.*

PART ONE

The Problem

During the Cuban missile crisis of October, 1962, a small knot of smugglers, including a half dozen Americans, watched the news from 29 Rue Bencharki in the casbah of Tangier. The Americans in the group had all been pro-Castro from the very beginning of the 1958 Cuban Revolution. But at the height of the crisis Junkie Gene expressed the feelings of the Americans: "Man, I've been against our policy with Cuba all along, but when Big Daddy says go, I go." Gene wanted to organize a European brigade to volunteer its services to the United States government.

On November 22, 1963, Big Daddy was killed by an assassin's bullet in Dallas, Texas. It will be generations before we can objectively survey the sociological and psychological impact that that momentous event had on the American people and particularly on the youth of the mid-1960's; but it is not too early for us to speculate a bit. Why, for instance, are the young people not rallying around President Johnson in the Vietnam War in the same way they were apparently about to rally around President Kennedy in the autumn of 1962? One can reply that it is a different type of war and Johnson is a different type of personality. True; but a full answer lies much deeper than that. Why did the first serious race riots occur the first summer after President Kennedy's death? What is this trend toward the kind of violence that has been erupting throughout the country since that infamous November day? Is it a deeply ingrained American sickness harking back to the frontier, as is so often alleged? There seems to be much more to it than this oversimplified guess. What of the more superficial but ostentatious signs of alienation or rebellion among our youth—the Beatle haircuts, the blurring sexual identity in their dress and in their idols of the entertainment and fashion worlds? Are these merely fads, or are they signs of something much deeper?

This book will begin by examining these questions. From there it will expand into the more vital question of the state of the American Revolution today. It will not be a kind book. It will step on the sensitivities of the entire political spectrum. By doing so, it is hoped that enough thought may be provoked to create more pragmatists in this world. For pragmatism, experimentation, compromise, and the humility to admit readily when we are wrong seem to offer the principal hopes for the nuclear age.

What we are experiencing in this country seems to be a combination of two sociological factors. The first one is simply that the people born after 1945, or those who were in their formative years in the early part of the nuclear age (the Truman and early Eisenhower years), have grown up. The pre-nuclear generations, including those born through the late thirties, have a profoundly different outlook toward life and death than those who remember nothing but a nuclear balance of terror. However ignorant the grade-school child or high-school student may be of the intricacies of world affairs, the possibility that next week may see the virtual end of the world, coupled with the virtual impossibility that he will live to the age predicted by the insurance tables, must always pervade his subconscious. This is bound to create a deep and sharp psychological difference between him and his elders; it is so sharp, in fact, that a completely different perspective toward life may be apparent in a particular community between a high-school class of 1956 and one of 1958. Violence frequently comes from fear. A frightened person may cringe and hide until he imagines he has been backed up as far as he can go, and then he will strike out at his persecutors, real or imagined. Or one can handle the threat of holocaust by simply trying not to think about it. Such a person must of course be careful not to put too much value on things, for things are not permanent. He must not take his family, education, or career too seriously. Tranquilizers and plenty of alcohol can help. These reactions to the nuclear threat are not unique to Americans. Naturally, because the United States controls the nuclear trigger, American society is one of the more highly criticized societies of the world. Innocent foreigners, who might also bear the full nuclear brunt of American foreign-policy mistakes, feel justifiably impotent when the United States moves in foreign affairs. Foreigners face annihilation without representation. It is meant as no apology for American errors in foreign affairs when the foreign reader is asked to consider for a moment how it might feel to be right under the nuclear umbrella rather than on its periphery. We elect the best leaders that we know how and that our machinery will permit us to elect. Sometimes our machinery leaves us with a choice of the lesser of two evils. Sometimes a leader in whom we have faith bewilders us. Improvement of political machinery to assure us of good leadership is what some of our more level-headed radicals want to accomplish. (Since the USSR became a nuclear power, in 1949, rational men have not been able to vote on domestic issues for the office of President in this country. The only question is which candidate is most likely to keep the world from nuclear war while maintaining independence and dignity for the United States as well as for those Western democracies that wish to throw in their lot with us. Race relations, farm problems, and poverty must take a back seat in presidential elections.) Most Americans are, at least between elections, nearly as helpless as, say, the Danes or the Australians with regard to our foreign-policy decisions. America today is a society built upon fear; and that fear is accentuated by our geographical position.

The second factor is the effects of the assassination. We are speaking here of the youth of America, but these effects are by no means confined to youth. And when we speak of youth in this connection, we must include not only the postwar genera-

tion but also those a half generation older, including many World
War II veterans and the "beat" literary school of Holmes, Mailer,
and Kerouac.

First let us look back before the assassination and try to understand what effect John F. Kennedy had upon these younger
citizens. We all know how fatherly, old President Eisenhower
provided reassurance for the American people. Certainly he had
a frightening foreign policy with John Foster Dulles as Secretary
of State for most of his administration; but Eisenhower himself
maintained his tranquility at times when Congress and the cabinet
lost theirs. He ended the Korean War just a few months after
taking office; and when in the Lebanon crisis of 1958, Congress
cried for extending and enlarging the draft, the President calmly
assured it that such legislation was not needed and proceeded
to settle the crisis without the loss of a single American life. Even
when relations between Soviet Premier Nikita Khrushchev and
President Eisenhower deteriorated to an unworkable state, everyone knew that a new President would be along in a short while.
Most importantly, no national trauma comparable to the Kennedy assassination occurred. Therefore the nuclear generation
grew up with some feeling of security, in spite of the over-all
threat of the bomb.

JFK took this younger generation by storm. His inaugural
address will go down as one of the great speeches in American
history. Norman Mailer felt after the President's death that for a
short time "we" were in power—meaning the American hipsters.
Kennedy erred only once on a major issue so far as most of
Mailer's "we" were concerned—in the 1961 Bay of Pigs invasion
of Cuba. It is only suggested here that the direction of that
error might be quite different from the direction for which
Kennedy was criticized by most of the American press at the
time; that is, perhaps he should have vetoed the operation in the
first place rather than provided more support. (The 1962 missile
crisis was a different matter. Here power politics and possible
future survival were at stake, and one could largely leave morals
and idealistic philosophizing aside.) Kennedy gradually re-

bounded from the unfortunate Bay of Pigs incident. His domestic successes were not notable, but he tried. He was diplomatic enough to get things done, but the times were not propitious for most of his pet domestic projects. When, however, the Test Ban Treaty with the Soviet Union was signed, the first major thaw in the cold war was a reality—a tremendous relief to those who fully comprehended the terrors of the nuclear age. Here was hope! One need not be beat any more! Here was youth and vitality; and the holocaust seemed much more remote than it had just a couple of short years before. Then Kennedy was shot down.

Who was at fault is not important for our purposes here. What is important is that what Dr. Timothy Leary describes as "the forces of middle-aged, middle-class authority" were back in control. Few people knew consciously, until the day of the assassination, what Kennedy had meant to them. A college freshman of today may not even realize that the assassination, which occurred when he was in junior high or early high school, had much effect on him at all. But it released the tremendous pent-up, subconscious fears of the nuclear generation. There was little hope now. Kennedy, who with his charming first lady cut such a dashing figure in diplomatic circles, was replaced by Lyndon Baines Johnson, the big hayseed from Texas who a scant thirty months earlier was jouncing about Asia making a general ass of himself —a trip which culminated in his famous illiterate camel-driver guest. And what were "we" offered the following autumn? Why, Johnson or Goldwater, of course. It was supposed to be a "real choice" for a change.

Not all of the nuclear generation wants a liberal government. On the contrary, many of those who are not apolitical out of sheer frustration are very extreme either on the Far Right or the Left. This, of course, is not universally true, but the trend is there. The new group of young Republicans is made up in large part of virulent, uncompromising reactionaries. Having organized themselves in such groups as the Young Americans for Freedom and having taken control of the Young Republicans, and if the Goldwater nomination is a guide, the Republican Party itself, they displayed their idea of democracy before a nationwide television audience when Governors Rockefeller and Romney tried to speak at the 1964 nominating convention.

On the other hand, we are developing in the so-called New Left a group of generally silly idealists. Being of a less practical nature, they seldom involve themselves in practical politics (although constant political discussion prevails among them), so that the young reactionaries tend to dominate the coming generation of prospective politicians. Because of this the threat to reason seems to be essentially from the Right. Both of these groups tend to disparage a middle-of-the-road position as being wishy-washy and lacking in commitment (which, I hope to show, is far from the case). As for the communists of the rob-and-rape-and-kill variety, they *are* frightening until one realizes how hard they are to find. So for practical purposes our discussion will be confined to those groups among the nuclear generation who actually exist in numbers.

The nuclear generation is in very serious danger of losing the ability to compromise. Signs of deteriorating into an extremism similar to that of many Latin-American countries abound. Attempts to blow up the Statue of Liberty and the Liberty Bell, the racial rioting, and of course the assassination are symptomatic. The youth of this country cannot stand many years of the current frustration until another John Kennedy comes along—someone who can promote world peace while maintaining American dignity. For until the nuclear generation finds its leader, we seem destined only to continue farther down the road toward chaos; and if that leader is not forthcoming, then for the survival of the American Revolution (which hopefully is still treasured among some youths) and very possibly for the survival of the world, we must grab ourselves by the bootstraps and cease our senseless, aimless tugging back and forth and regain our direction.

The moderate position is not a glamorous one. The reader will note, for instance, that there are less likely to be movie stars, astronauts, or Grand Prix race drivers among moderate candidates for office. Most moderates[1] tend to be practical, workaday politicians. A movie star can, of course, be a good legislator or administrator. But when a definite trend toward such glamor candidates is established, as in California, it is an indication that the drift toward extremism may already have advanced to a dangerous stage.

If it is not clear by now, this essay is a defense of, nay, an appeal for, the middle of the road in American politics. And at the risk of alienating all but the already committed moderate, I have laid the groundwork by insulting extremists of both Right and Left. This is unavoidable. The primary job of a pragmatic political writer is to shake people loose from their uncompromising dogmas rather than to gain agreement with every one of his ideas. I hope to show before I am through that the Declaration of Independ-

---

[1] The term *moderate* is used throughout to mean one with a pragmatic outlook and not so wedded to ideology that he cannot deviate from his philosophical base on most issues. Although currently the term is popularly applied to members of the one major political party more frequently than to members of the other, it is not so used here. Most of the non-southern Democrats and such "liberal" Republicans as Senator Jacob Javits, then, are all moderates. For the purposes of this book, the terms *conservative*, *middle-of-the-road*, and *liberal* merely indicate three bands in the moderate spectrum. Conservative would also describe Senator Javits, whose philosophical base is laissez faire, even though he pragmatically deviates from dogma sufficiently to be considered a Republican liberal by most observers. Liberal might best be personified by Vice-President Humphrey. He is usually, but not always, in favor of big spending. His philosophical base is Keynesian (even though he may often forget that Keynes recommended a budgetary surplus in days of prosperity). Humphrey can be somewhat conservative in practice. The term *reactionary* will generally be used to describe those who are frequently called conservative in popular usage. Some reactionaries would resort to violent means to achieve their goals; others simply may not understand or accept the Bill of Rights. Hence an individual who would deny full constitutional rights to the Negro would be something of a reactionary, even though he might be liberal in many other respects.

Two political classifications which are not currently represented in Congress are *socialist* and *radical*. A socialist is herein defined as one who is committed to government ownership of property through constitutional means. A radical is one who would use violent or unconstitutional means to obtain liberal or socialist ends. The term radical includes true communists.

ence is a great socialist doctrine and that extremism in the defense of liberty is *not* a vice. I will review the American Revolution and chastise the New Left and the socialists for allowing themselves to be alienated from that revolution while feebly standing aside as conservatives and reactionaries tell them that the Revolution somehow does not belong to them while they accept the myth that American democracy is compatible with only laissez faire. I will also castigate the reactionaries for presuming that they have exclusive claim to the Constitution, while only giving lip service to that document so far as regards sharing it with their fellow Americans who advocate a different economic system. I will try to show that both socialists and conservatives are wasting their time on ideology by debating who would own what, rather than what use wealth and property shall be put to. For as we should all know by examining past and present experiences in this country, Britain, Scandinavia, and Latin America, privately owned but government-controlled industry (such as this nation's railroads) does not necessarily guarantee the stockholder an unreasonable profit; and public ownership of land, as evidenced by much of the land reform in Latin America, does not in any way guarantee an efficient use of that property. I will point to some startling parallels between nineteenth-century German history and twentieth-century American history. I will try to point out to all dogmatists the absurdity of carrying most positions to their logical conclusions. I hope to put the political climate of the late 1960's into some sort of historical perspective, both nationally and internationally.

Thus you will find me in the position of advocating the right of private property and referring to the words of John Locke on this subject, while on the other hand encouraging reasonable socialists to participate in the democratic processes we have established. The pragmatist, if he suddenly found himself in the imaginary position of administering ten different countries running the gamut of the political spectrum, would start with ten different bases rather than one as the dogmatist would. Our pragmatist would change each individual country as needed until they would all probably approach the middle of the political spectrum.

This may sound to some readers as if the moderate will not fight for what he believes to be right. This is not at all true. To an American moderate, for instance, certainly the Four Freedoms (and perhaps the freedom of morals[2]) are worth fighting for. The key is being able to distinguish between what is worth fighting for and what is negotiable. But for the moderate to enable himself to negotiate, he must first persuade the dogmatist to be less dogmatic and to negotiate with him. Only then can we get down to the business of survival in the nuclear age.

Somewhere along the line the further-left American liberal and the socialist became alienated from the political life of the country. Liberals, in the sense of the classical European Liberalism of the two previous centuries, have frequently been an idealistic lot. In Germany, in 1848, they held a constitutional convention in Frankfurt but failed to make any moves to seize control of the army, thereby dooming their revolution to failure.[3] In postwar United States many leftists seemed to accept the reactionary line that this country and system of government did not belong to them. Thus the New Left does not generally concern itself with practical adult politics, but rather contents itself with casting protest votes, marching and picketing (which are fine as far as they go) and dabbling in campus politics, which is essentially child's play. A case in point occurred in Bloomington, Indiana, in June, 1967. The local police had suddenly adopted the policy of asking students who congregated in groups or stopped to chat to move on or be arrested for loitering. Naturally, after a very few days of this, a stand-in was organized and consequently a number

---

[2] By *freedom of morals* is meant not license to do completely as one pleases, but rather the concept that one should be free to do as he pleases unless he *directly* infringes on the property or rights of another. Sexual freedom, pot smoking, and the like would generally be protected by constitutional guarantees, while assault and battery, theft, and destruction of property would remain violations of the law.

[3] See pp. 53 ff.

of students were arrested. Bloomington had a Republican mayor (who appoints the chief of police) and during the fracas someone commented that perhaps the city needed a Democratic mayor after the approaching election. Another student gave the unfortunate position of the New Left by replying that Bloomington needed a "Democratic Society" (a reference to the leftist Students for a Democratic Society). Of course Bloomington needs a democratic society; but the citizens are not about to get one by the forsaking of traditional politics, which was implied in the reference to the "Democratic Society." Where are the student registration drives and the student candidates?[4]

At approximately the same time that the American Negro has finally gained his manhood, most white American leftists have lost theirs. If they do not like the candidates which either of the two major political parties offers, they will remain completely outside those parties and hence the American political system. The leftist can have no influence in America today by remaining radical. The American Revolution is one of the hippest revolutions in the history of the world. The Thirteen Colonies stood up to Great Britain and said in essence, "We've had enough!"—in the same manner that Cuba stood up to the United States in recent years and in the same manner that the American Negro is finally standing up to his white oppressors. The Declaration of Independence calls for the rights to "life, liberty, and the pursuit of happiness." The right to life! That means enough to eat and a roof over one's head. The pursuit of happiness should certainly include an education for one's children in this wealthy country. But the starry-eyed New Left lets the reactionaries tell them that the country doesn't belong to them. There is yet no need for a call to arms; there is rather a need for all men to exercise freedom of speech and the right to vote, and to defend these with their very lives if other means fail completely.

The term *moderate*, as used in this book, means virtually any American who supports the Constitution of the United States, whether he is of liberal or conservative bent. This definition

---

[4] In fairness to the city of Bloomington and the current administration, it must be said that such incidents as the one just related are extremely rare.

leaves a surprising number outside its scope, including many reactionary congressmen. There are those, for instance, who would ban overt dissent on the Vietnam War, at least partly on the ground that it gives aid and comfort to the enemy. Those who would squelch dissent place themselves in the unfortunate position of trying to outlaw the very freedom that they say we are fighting for in that distant war. For if these people truly treasured the American freedoms, they would encourage free and open dissent, and if Ho Chi Minh and those around him misinterpreted the debate, that must be their misfortune—they must suffer the consequences. (We must be on guard against a declaration of war by Congress in this or any other limited war. Such an act could immediately change dissenters into traitors and could be the basis for a totalitarian takeover.) It is not the responsibility of the American people to educate the enemy in the ways of a free society while we are at war. We must leave our society intact and fight the war, if continue we must, within the framework of that society. It is hardly a fair exchange to force democracy upon others while losing our freedoms at home. (We should all know by now that the actual reasons for American participation in the Vietnam War have absolutely nothing to do with freedom for Vietnam: the issue is the security of the United States and her allies. Talk of concern for the freedom of South Vietnam only clouds the real issues and is a notorious example of the unfortunate moralism which has been a part of United States foreign policy throughout the nation's existence. The problem reaches terrifying proportions in the nuclear age. With this moralistic approach we seem incapable of being honest with ourselves, and we tend to lose sight of our goals.) Congressional reactionaries thus place themselves in the position of being strong enemies of freedom. It doesn't seem that matters would be improved by electing radicals to Congress as well. Our problem will be solved, not by adding another evil, but rather by discrediting the reactionaries.

PART TWO

The Historical Perspective

This is not a history of freedom, nor do I profess to be enough of a historian to be able to write one. But a review of some of the major trends and events in the European world from the Italian Renaissance onward will be useful here. The Renaissance was a reaction to the Middle Ages. It was important primarily because it was a period of breaking away from centuries of stagnation. The breaking away from convention gave way to grotesqueness. Palmer and Colton, authors of a standard college text in world history, speak of the Renaissance as follows:

> The humanists not only steeped themselves in antiquity . . . They disdained to write in Italian, as earlier writers like Dante and Boccaccio had done. They scoffed at the current Latin used in the church and the universities . . . all medieval Latin was dismissed by the humanists as barbarous and corrupted. It was only with the vocabulary and style of a Cicero or a Vergil that the humanists would consent to write. We hear of one churchman who made a habit of washing his mouth after saying mass, because he considered the Latin of the mass to be so debased. In their effort to write exactly like ancients, the humanists naturally made it impossible for themselves to treat most contemporary questions. They sacrificed matter to manner, and content to verbal effects. They astonished each other with feats of stylistic *virtu*, but they seemed never to learn what seems so obvious: that the Greeks and Romans had not been simply mere imitators, and that the classic virtues have never included imitation, however ingenious. . . .

... The Renaissance was a movement of the elite. It was not exactly aristocratic, because aristocracy implies a concern with birth and background to which Italians of the Renaissance were largely indifferent; but it was exclusive in spirit, affecting a small group of acutely self-conscious persons at the top of society, or those who by their *virtu* might reach the top. Renaissance individualism was the individualism of the dazzling few. The pomposities of the humanists were mocked by the populace in their own day. The humanists, by insisting on an artificial elaborateness, made writing a new kind of mystery of which they alone were the masters. When printing, invented in Germany about 1450, began to spread into Italy the Italian humanists received it with indignation. Printed books seemed a cheap substitute for their beloved manuscripts, nor did they wish any enlargement of the reading public to include persons without taste. Taste, style, manner, correctitude, *aplomb* were set above more substantial attainments.[1]

While we can chuckle at these humanists with their affected reaction to the Middle Ages, it is easy to see similarities between them and today's hippies and their reaction to puritanism. (We find, if we look around, that countries which have deep moralistic streaks running through them tend to overreact, just as the humanists reacted to the Middle Ages. Catholic countries frequently lean toward communism, either as a form of government, a large party as in Italy, or an underground movement. By the same token, the excesses of the hippie movement would probably not exist if it weren't for puritanism. Psychologically, it is probably the retention of the moralistic streak in the make-up of many of these people which causes them to go quickly from one extreme to the other without feeling their way first through the middle.)

What is usually thought of as puritanism in this country is really a bit of Bible-belt southern or rural old-fashioned Protestantism. Except in the smallest communities, for instance, a man can usually live with a mistress if he wishes to or say "fuck" virtually whenever he pleases. If, however, he insists on carrying a sign that advertises, "I'm living with a young lady out of wedlock!"

[1] R. R. Palmer and Joel Colton, *A History of the Modern World,* 3rd ed. (New York: Knopf), pp. 53, 54.

or "fuck," he has a very good chance of finding what little puritanism might be left. Not that such an encounter might not offer some occasional sport; but there are more important things to tackle.[2] (These types of demonstrations might have had more validity even ten years ago. Now that puritanism may be essentially dead,[3] it seems that the junior beatniks have decided to challenge the minority of crabs that remain instead of moving on to new fields.) The difference between the two attitudes toward freedom —both groups doing as they please, but one making a show of its differences, while the other quietly goes about its business trying less ostentatiously to change things for the better—is the difference between impotent anger and progress, or between the Red and the liberal. These two may not differ much in the ends they desire, but the one offends established society with his unpolitical manners to such an extent that it is little wonder the Reds were driven underground years ago, while the other works toward his goals usually with some success.

As for the free-speech movement, it has some relation to freedom of morals. And freedom of morals *is* an important issue; however, it is essentially a *new* one. It is ridiculous to revolt immediately in an angry manner until the established processes are given an adequate chance. It is amazing to note that issues that were spoken of only by the avant-garde a short ten years ago are discussed seriously in every rural community in the country today—legalized abortion, sexual and moral freedom, legalization of pot, mass racial integration—the list is endless. These fantastic inroads are evidenced by new legislation and concern in all fields. The system, in fact, is working at a faster pace

[2] We are witnessing a major change in swearing in the English language. Words which refer to sexual acts and acts of elimination, and which were our lowest swear words a generation ago, are now used freely in mixed company among the hip segments of the avant-garde. They are being replaced by racial slurs, such as *nigger* and *wop*, which are not acceptable, in most contexts, among these same people. If the Berkeley free-speech movement had wanted a real challenge, they should have carried a sign to the colored district of Oakland reading "Nigger!"

[3] This is only personal opinion; the subject would make an interesting sociological study.

than ever before. The older generation is living up to their responsibility to change. The great problem seems to be now that the younger generation is not giving proper credit where credit is due. But youth, always impatient, demands even faster change than we have today.

A major cause of the impatience of youth stems out of an unavoidable lack of historical perspective. So, if you will, let us return to the past. After the Renaissance came the rise of the modern nation-state and the golden age of monarchy. We will not dwell on this particular period except to note that the distinction between East and West became clearer here. In a historical sense Eastern Europe included Austria, Scandinavia, and much of Germany, while Western Europe was considered to be France, Britain (although a lack of communications kept events in England from being widely followed on the Continent), the Netherlands, Iberia, and Italy. Originally the division was made by political thinkers along the line which separated the jurisdictional areas of the Roman Catholic and Greek Orthodox churches. As the Western countries developed into nation-states, ridded themselves of medieval institutions, such as serfdom, and granted some power to nobles and burghers, the Eastern group remained behind.

Well into the nineteenth century, geographers could draw an approximate line through Europe which divided that continent into two areas—that where serfdom still reigned and that where it was non-existent or took on forms in which the serf was more nearly free. This line ran through Germany. Prussia, with Berlin as its capital, was included in the area of serfdom. Serfdom was officially abolished in Prussia in 1807 under Napoleonic (Western) influence, but it remained in practice until much later. The serfs were finally freed in Russia in 1861.

The first modern revolution of importance today to the European world was known as the Glorious Revolution of 1688. It occurred in England and was actually the compromise following an extended period of chaos which included a civil war, a regicide, a military dictatorship, and a restoration which lasted for only twenty-eight years and two kings. It began a string of revolutions which includes the American, French, Latin-American and communist revolutions of the twentieth century. The essential problem in 1688 was a religious one. Parliament, which had developed peacefully over the centuries in England, as had parliaments in some other countries, as a gathering of nobles to whom the king would appeal for funds and taxes and whom the king would inform of matters important to them, gained power slowly. James II, 1685–88, had strong Catholic leanings, and antagonized both the Whigs and the Tories—the Tories having been loyal to the crown up until James's reign. Parliament offered the throne to the Dutchman, William of Orange, and his wife Mary. William invaded England with a large army; James fled, and the Glorious Revolution was almost an accomplished fact. What remained to be done was to define the relationship between the Crown and Parliament—and this is important, for remember that revolutions are seldom successful without well-defined goals. A Bill of Rights affirming the rights of petition, the bearing of arms, habeas corpus, upholding freedom of debate, requiring the king to obtain consent of Parliament before he could have a standing army, specifying he must be a Protestant, and depriving him of the power to suspend the laws, was signed by King William in 1689. Acts regarding the military, the duration of Parliament, and the legal rights of those accused of treason ensued; and the Act of Settlement of 1701 specified that the crown should descend to Anne, Mary's younger sister. All are properly regarded as part of the revolutionary settlement. Note that the English did maintain their basic institutions—the crown, Parliament, property, the aristocracy, and their venerable system of law. The revolution was for specific ends which were obtained in the acts listed above.

Most Americans are familiar with John Locke. Locke, whose major works were published in 1690, was the "glorifier" of the 1688 Revolution. He gave it its philosophical basis and with it the basis for the American and French revolutions of the next century. This is not the place to delve into the concept that government derives its just powers from the consent of the governed, which is reflected in the Declaration of Independence (a document which essentially reflects the thoughts of John Locke as translated by Thomas Jefferson). What our revolutionary documents, including the Constitution, do ignore in Locke's philosophy is a point that has become sorely debated today: What is the role of property with regard to the American Revolution? The quote is from Locke's *Second Treatise on Civil Government*:

OF PROPERTY

God, who hath given the world to men in common, hath also given them reason to make use of it to the best advantage of life and convenience. The earth and all that is therein is given to men for the support and comfort of their being. And though all the fruits it naturally produces, and beasts it feeds, belong to mankind in common, as they are produced by the spontaneous hand of nature, and no body has originally a private dominion exclusive of the rest of mankind in any of them, as they are thus in their natural state, yet being given for the use of men, there must of necessity be a means to appropriate them some way or other, before they can be of any use, or at all beneficial, to any particular man. The fruit or venison which nourishes the wild Indian, who knows no enclosure, and is still a tenant in common, must be his, and so his—i.e., a part of him, that another can no longer have any right to it before it can do him any good for the support of his life.

Though the earth and all inferior creatures be common to all men, yet every man has a *property* in his own *person*. This nobody has any right to but himself. The *labour* of his body and the *work* of his hand, we may say, are properly his. Whatsoever, then, he removes out of the state that nature has provided and left it in, he hath mixed his labour with it, and joined to it something that is his own, and thereby makes it his property. . . .

He that is nourished by the acorns he picked up under an oak, or the apples he gathered from the trees in the wood, has certainly appropriated them to himself. Nobody can deny but that the nourishment is his. I ask, then, when did they begin to be his? when he digested? or when he ate? or when he boiled? or when he brought them home? or when he picked them up? And 'tis plain if the first gathering made them not his, nothing else could. That labour put a distinction between them and common. That added something to them more than Nature, the common mother of all, had done, and so they became his private right. . . .

It will perhaps be objected to this, that if gathering the acorns or other fruits of the earth, etc., makes a right to them, then any one may engross as much as he will. To which I answer, Not so. The same law of nature that does by this means give us property, does also bound that property too. *God has given us all things richly, I Tim. vi 12.* Is the voice of reason confirmed by inspiration? But how far has he given it to us, *to enjoy?* As much as any one can make use of to any advantage of life before it spoils, so much he may by his labour fix a property in. Whatever is beyond this is more than his share, and belongs to others. . . .

But the chief matter of property being now not the fruits of the earth, and the beasts that subsist on it, but the earth itself, as that which takes in and carries all the rest, I think it is plain that property in that too is acquired as the former. As much land as a man tills, plants, improves, cultivates, and can use the product of, so much is his property. . . .

OF THE ENDS OF POLITICAL SOCIETY AND GOVERNMENT

If man in the state of nature can be so free as has been said; if he be absolute lord of his own person and possessions; equal to the greatest and subject to no body, why will he part with his freedom? Why will he give up this empire, and subject himself to the dominion and control of any other power? To which 'tis obvious to answer, that though in the state of nature he hath such a right, yet the enjoyment of it is very uncertain and constantly exposed to the invasion of others; for all being kings as much as he, every man his equal, and the greater part no strict observers of equity and justice, the enjoyment of the property he has in this state is very unsafe, very insecure. This makes him willing to quit this condition which, however free, is full of fears and continual dangers; and 'tis not without reason that he seeks out and is willing to join in society with others who are already united, or have a mind to unite for the mutual preservation of their lives, liberties, and estates, which I call by the general name, property.

The great and chief end therefore, of men's uniting into com-
monwealths, and putting themselves under government, is the
preservation of their property; to which in the state of nature
there are many things wanting. . . .[4]

Thus politically began the Age of Enlightenment—the greatest
period of thought in the history of the modern world. And thus
were the philosophical seeds planted for the American Revolution,
a direct product of the Enlightenment. Locke would, it seems,
defend and probably fight for private property. But he would also
probably support just as strongly the duty of government to
maintain controls over property to ensure that ownership of property is not abused—that no man retains more property than he can
reasonably use before it spoils. The philosophical basis for such
measures as the progressive income tax, anti-trust laws, the doctrine of public utility, the right of eminent domain, all seem im-
plicit here within a basic framework of private property. We shall
discuss the concept of laissez faire below as well as the question
whether the failure of laissez faire to work when carried to an
extreme implies a failure of the system of private property and
classical Liberalism.[5]

The Liberal confidence in man's power of self-government is
overshadowed today by attempts to patronize the citizen as if he

---

[4] Ludwig F. Schaefer, David H. Fowler, Jacob E. Cook (editors),
Problems in Western Civilization (New York: Scribner's, 1966). From *The
Works of John Locke* (London, 1801), Vol. V, pp. 353-56.

[5] Classical Liberalism is a concept of the Enlightenment. Liberals had
confidence in man's power of self-government, reasonable discussion, and
ability to legislate. They demanded full disclosure of all actions of government. They were opposed to universal manhood suffrage, for they feared
excesses in mob rule. They adopted the laissez faire of the British Manchester school of economics, both domestically and internationally, and so
were generally free traders and against the old system of mercantilism or
government control of foreign trade. They frowned on established churches
and landed aristocracies and favored freedom of religion. In spite of suffrage differences, the American Revolution is a Liberal revolution. The
nearest thing to a classical Liberal today in the United States is a moderate-
conservative. A liberal in the sense of contemporary American politics will
be differentiated from the classical Liberal by the use of the capital *L*
in the latter case throughout this book.

were incapable of deciding himself what is best for him. When this elevation of the state above the individual is carried to an extreme, totalitarianism results, as we shall see. One should also note the trend toward secrecy in government and how this conflicts with Liberal thinking.

Since it can be assumed that most readers are generally familiar with the American Revolution, we shall turn instead to the French Revolution, which began in 1789. It is my opinion that the French Revolution is extremely overrated by historians, not in general importance but in its relation to freedom. The French Revolution was no doubt an outgrowth of the American. Just as the Russian Revolution more than a century later failed miserably, if success is measured by the achievement of the desires of the majority of those who began the revolution, the French Revolution never achieved its Liberal goals. The failure resulted in the Napoleonic Wars and a disastrous defeat for France. Before Napoleon appeared on the scene, France managed nothing but a series of successive attempts at government which were marked by a virtually endless stream of blood. Our task is not to examine the events of the French Revolution in detail but to try to discover why it failed. To do so, we must enlist the aid of Edmund Burke (d. 1797).

Edmund Burke was a conservative member of Parliament during the American and French revolutions. Conservative though he was, however, he did not oppose change. He was philosophically opposed to both of these revolutions, nevertheless, and consequently his views are probably not given enough thought by American students. He did support the American colonies against the British Parliament in their stand against taxation, and he naturally supported the English Revolution of 1688. If we examine his reasoning carefully, we find that his thinking is not inconsistent.

Burke's distinction was this. The English Bill of Rights (the equivalent of the American Constitution in this case) stated exactly what Parliament intended to gain from the revolution. As mentioned earlier, the English retained the basic institutions upon which their centuries-old society was built. At the time of the war with the American colonies, the Americans had not yet declared their goals. (The Constitution was not adopted until 1787 and the Bill of Rights until 1789.) We were fortunate that the men who founded our nation were able to work things out through compromise. How fortunate we were can be seen by the unpleasant example of the French Revolution. The only major document issued by the French at the outbreak of strife in 1789 was the Declaration of the Rights of Man. This was an idealistic document similar to our Declaration of Independence. No document comparable to our Constitution and the English Bill of Rights was promulgated. Burke was immediately alarmed by the French Revolution because no stated goals at all were promulgated by the French revolutionaries. Burke wrote *Reflections on the Revolution in France* and became the correct prophet of doom in much the same way as did Winston Churchill a century and a half later. Burke dryly pointed out that if we permit individuals to do as they please, "we ought to see what it will please them to do before we risk congratulations." Willcox puts Burke's philosophy well:

... He recognized the truth of the old adage that times change and we change with them, and he had made his name as a reformer; but he insisted that reform must not be the means of eliminating the good with the bad. He was too much pervaded by a sense of the past to be a revolutionary. The social organism for him was not a thing of the moment, to be reconstituted according to the dictates of abstract philosophy; it was the product of a slow and infinitely complex process of historical development, "a partnership not only between those who are living, but between those who are living, those who are dead, and those who are to be born." The revolutionary would dissolve the partnership and destroy the organism in the hope of creating something better in its place. The French were denying their past for the sake of an untried future, and their faith that reason alone could create utopia struck Burke as madness.[6]

Burke expresses the philosophy of today's moderate—the so-

⁶ William B. Willcox, *The Age of Aristocracy, 1688 to 1830* (Boston: Heath, 1966), p. 151.

called middle-of-the-roader. To bring our discussion to the present, let us try to imagine what a young American man who had wholeheartedly adopted Burke's philosophy might be like today. The key word here is *sophistication,* in a very special sense. To illustrate, let us suppose our young man comes from a middle-class Southern Baptist family, is educated in business and Russian studies at a large midwestern state university, and travels to Europe and Asia after graduation. Let us further suppose that he is a thinking man and has been able to set aside deliberately all that he was taught as a child, but only temporarily for examination purposes. His friends during this period will probably come mainly from the New Left, but he still maintains contact with friends from home and the business school, as well as his family. Perhaps he will grow a beard, wear long hair, smoke pot, read Marx on economics and Philip Wylie on religion. Most of his friends from the New Left are "Europe worshipers" who imagine that all things are better in Europe. To them, everything American is bad—even the food. They generalize about Europe while their generalizations may be true of only France or Germany. Eventually our hypothetical young man integrates himself. He realizes through his reading and his association with Negro and liberal friends that there is no rational basis whatsoever for persecution of the Negro, and that the reason the American Negro took one hundred years to "become American" is that his people were the victims of the most degrading system of slavery known to history—that to imagine the Negro should have acted like the freedom-conscious American white and asserted his rights at the time of emancipation is only to substitute the experience of his own race for that of the Negro.[7] He becomes active in civil-rights work on a more permanent basis. As a member of SNCC during the recent shift in emphasis, he will probably remain active as long as he conscientiously can in an effort to moderate the organization. He does not support riots but believes in self-defense. He contributes to the Deacons for Defense and Justice in Louisiana but does not support Negro racist organizations, such as the

_____
[7] For a brilliant comparative study of American slavery, see Stanley J. Elkins, *Slavery* (Chicago: Univ. of Chicago Press, 1959).

Black Muslims. He has gone through a period of naive atheism and has decided that there is more to the universe than that doctrine offers. He cannot return to conventional Christianity; he has read the Vedas and Zen philosophy and perhaps ends up in the Unitarian church. He eventually gets his hair cut but keeps his beard for a while until he takes a job demanding that he be clean-shaven. He supports the goals of the now defunct Fair Play for Cuba Committee, even though it was organized by Trotskyites, with whom he has major differences; for he sincerely believes that Cuba was pushed toward her present position by unfortunate United States policy. He will temporarily discard many habits, for practical reasons, which are completely foreign to the society in which he lives. But he retains an occasional foreign mannerism, such as the European style of silverware manipulation, because he finds it easier, and he remains unassuming about these minor differences. He decides that he likes American meat loaf after all, along with hamburgers, ice cream, and grits. He finds French cooking overrated but has two or three favorite French dishes. He is proud to be an American but freely criticizes his country if he feels it deserves criticism. He is on good relations with his family and retains a few good friends in the small southern town where he was reared. He is a fiscal conservative because his courses in economics led him to a concern about the balance of payments. He may support the Vietnam War—not because he feels it is moral but because he accepts the domino theory. But he does none of these things out of affectation. A stranger might notice nothing different about him from any other educated southerner. His sophistication will permit him neither to rebel for the sheer sake of rebelling nor to conform merely for the sake of conforming. He will take the good and discard the bad, in his judgment, by examining each and every issue on its individual merits. And he will proudly defend his right to be an individual both to those who believe that a strong civil-rights advocate must necessarily be against the Vietnam War and to those who believe that a fiscal conservative must support United States Cuban policy. He cannot understand how any thinking man could ally himself with either right or left on all issues. And as such, he is much more of an individual than dogmatists of the Young Americans for Freedom or of the New Left (the latter seeming to lack ability to see anything good about their society). The degeneration of American politics into two opposed dogmatic positions actually indicates a lack of individualism in partisans of both extremes.

Our hypothetical friend is much like Edmund Burke. *Reform must not be the means of eliminating the good with the bad.*

The Napoleonic occupation brought the twin reactions, nationalism and romanticism, to Europe (neither ism being what Americans today are likely to think it is). Nationalism was directed toward finding one's national identity, usually but not necessarily based upon a language. It had nothing to do with expansionism, except when one's concept of "natural boundaries" was different from existing political boundaries. It was more akin to today's Black Nationalism than the nationalism Americans think of when they talk of winning a foreign war. It meant developing the literature, music, and other cultural elements of a people in order to distinguish themselves from other national groups, and it frequently entailed developing a written language for the first time.

Romanticism comes from the same source. In many ways it *is* nationalism. In English-speaking countries, romanticism is generally thought to be a harmless literary movement. The romantic literature we are familiar with in English, involving a certain style, and investigating the nature of truth, the relation of man to his universe, and the value of feeling, is just a peripheral part of the romantic movement. The core of romanticism was in Germany. Its basic philosophy failed to have tremendous political appeal outside of German-speaking lands; it was a reaction to the Enlightenment and the Age of Reason as well as to Napoleon, and it was the forerunner of Nazism.

German romanticism found the rationalism of the Enlightenment insipid. It longed for passion—the more the better. Thus the irrational rather than the rational was sought. German romanticists found their inspiration in the Middle Ages; the con-

temporary world was repulsive to them and inspiration lay in
history. They found it quite natural to confuse history and poetry.
Without any immediate hope of national unification—Germany
was only an area with a common language divided into many
small principalities—Germans sought the identity of the fatherland
(nationalism) in the glorious days of the barbaric conquests
of Rome and the rest of Europe. The romanticists of this early
period—Novalis (pen name of Friedrich von Hardenberg), August
Wilhelm, Friedrich von Schlegel, and above all Adam Müller
(d. 1849), the chief political philosopher of the movement—felt
that the German people were possessed of a kind of manifest
destiny to repeat their era of barbaric, militaristic greatness. Although political unification was far from a universal goal of the
Germans, romanticism found its ultimate goal in the nation.
Germany had been left behind by the Western countries in the
formation of a modern nation-state, for she had been unable to
unite, and with the exception of Austria, she consequently was
militarily weak for centuries.

The state became the ultimate goal of society. The Western
countries, with their dangerous concept of subverting the state
to the individual, became objects of scorn. Capitalism was only
a tool for such an end. The good of the state was the proper
goal of all good Germans, and everything, including commerce,
was to be directed toward that end. Nor could the state afford
to absorb inferior peoples, even those already within its boundaries. In this way the seeds of National Socialism were planted.[8]

One of the connecting links of the early nineteenth and mid-
twentieth centuries in German history was a movement, the roots
of which are described above, called "the war against the West"
which was personified by a character known as Father Jahn.
For a description of Jahn, we turn to Pinson:

> Friedrich Ludwig Jahn [d. 1852], known as Turnvater Jahn,
> had already before 1815 achieved fame and notoriety by the
> organization of his *Turngemeinden,* or sport associations. He urged

---

[8] For a discussion of German romanticism, see especially Hans Kohn,
The Mind of Germany (New York: Scribner's, 1960). This is *the* English
language's intellectual history of Germany.

the physical and national regeneration of German youth for the cause of the fatherland. His was a combination of moral idealism and crude and vulgar rowdyism, of folk populism and antisemitism, of racialism and patriotism. The wearing of gray shirts, which he prescribed for his followers, was intended to break down class distinctions and create a feeling of national unity in all who wore them. But they are also a sinister anticipation of the twentieth century brown shirts. *Similarly so was also the rowdyism with which Jahn's followers invaded the universities and broke up the classes and lectures of professors whom they considered antinational.* In 1811 Jahn had submitted to the rector of the University of Berlin a plan for the formation of the Burschenschaften [student associations formed to promote patriotism, Christian conduct, and Liberal ideas] to supplant the organization of students along state lines. The plan was rejected at that time. But in Jena . . . the first Burschenschaft was formed on June 12, 1851, under the slogan of "Honor, Liberty and Fatherland," with the two fold goal of national unity and the strengthening of moral virtues. . . .[9]

Jahn glorified his native Prussia, but later switched his allegiance to Germany. (He was one of the delegates to the Frankfurt Assembly of 1848, which attempted to unite Germany under a Liberal constitution.) Kohn describes Jahn's influence further:

. . . In 1806 he wrote the first draft of his *Deutsches Volkstum* which appeared in 1810. This is one of the essential books for an understanding of the new nationalism. In it the influence of romanticism combined with that of the French Revolution and of the Prussian traditions; of the three elements the romantic prevailed: the emphasis was no longer on the citizen in a society founded on law nor on the loyalty of the subject to his hereditary monarch, but *on the originality of a deeply rooted creative force, the German Volk.*

Here was an almost mystical force that transcended mere history; it became for Jahn one of the central and elemental forces of nature and a supreme part of God's own creative effort. Jahn did not confine himself to developing the theory of folkdom; during the crucial years of the formation of German nationalism

---

[9] Koppel S. Pinson, *Modern Germany: Its History and Civilization* (New York: Macmillan, 1954), p. 63. (Italics mine.)

he became its indefatigable propagandist. Most important was his influence on three movements which were not only characteristic of German nationalism but models as well for similar trends in central and eastern Europe: free corps of patriotic volunteers; gymnastic associations for the training of patriotic fighters; and student fraternities aflame with nationalistic zeal. Each of these three movements stood in its own peculiar way for freedom—but a freedom overcharged with nationalistic emotionalism and stressing the disciplined dedication to national service, *a freedom which had little in common with the Western concepts of individual liberty*.[10] [Italics mine.]

We have called the Enlightenment "the greatest period of thought in the history of the modern world," while generally disparaging romanticism.[11] But did romanticism have no saving graces? Was there perhaps some shortcoming or flaw in the philosophy of the Enlightenment which made rebellion from its philosophy reasonable, in spite of the grotesque form of romanticism? The answer is, Yes, there was such a flaw. The thinkers of the Enlightenment held that we live in an orderly universe. Nature, it was felt, was a great master plan. Man, if he could only find his place within this orderly universe and thus regulate his society, would find happiness. The romanticists pointed to the barbarity of man, death, disease, famine, pestilence, and all other misfortunes which it is the purpose of life to avoid. Voltaire's classic *Candide* beautifully satirized the concept of the orderly universe. What developed, however, was not an improvement over the Enlightenment but a school of thought which irrationally discarded the entire basis of the previous philosophy. The Enlightenment put forward the concept of the cosmos, and the romanticists felt that the universe was chaos. Today the LSD experience, if a successful experience, leaves one in basic agreement with the philosophy of the Enlightenment—that there is order and beauty within the universe; but before a person under acid is able to see the cosmos, he may have to experience an unimaginable amount of psychic chaos. The key here, and the key to the reconciliation of the two schools of thought, can best be illustrated by the famous serenity

[10] Kohn, *op. cit.*, pp. 82-83.
[11] See pp. 49, 50.

prayer (adopted by Alcoholics Anonymous): "God grant me the serenity to accept the things I cannot change, courage to change the things I can, and wisdom to know the difference." Extremists of the Enlightenment felt that man could and should control everything. The romanticists observed that no matter how hard man tried or believed in his orderly universe, he sometimes was impotent to prevent disaster from befalling him. As man seems to have the unfortunate tendency to carry all things to ridiculous extremes, the romanticists eventually perverted the simple truth that man could never control any part of his environment. This became the basis for acceptance of the barbarities of Nazi Germany and nuclear war. As we shall see, romanticism is very much with us in America today. The romanticists actually had some valid disagreement with extremists of the Enlightenment, for as every movement has its extremists, some of the writers of the Enlightenment tended to become a bit silly. As for who was right, the Enlightened thinkers or the romanticists, one can only pragmatically observe that when man believed his universe to be orderly and held the power to control it, he did a much better, albeit imperfect, job of controlling it than when he had tended to feel that his universe controlled him. The romantic philosophy fed upon the fact that the Enlightenment was not perfect. (Opposing philosophies, such as capitalism and socialism, romantically feed upon the imperfections of each other in the same way. Obviously no system of government, economics, or philosophy will ever achieve the perfection mankind seems to long for. But imperfection is *not* failure.) By the same token the acid experience teaches one that chaos and orderliness coexist in the universe. The twentieth century has yet to devise a major school of thought to replace romanticism. The negativism of existentialism, nihilism, and beat is only an expression of acceptance of this extreme romanticism. While the Enlightenment stressed the courage to change the things we can, romanticism dwelled upon the acceptance of the things we cannot change. The task of the current generation of thinkers is to develop the wisdom to know the difference.

The first serious attempt to unite Germany in the nineteenth century was a Liberal attempt, culminating in the Frankfurt Assembly of 1848–49. Liberals abounded in Germany in the nineteenth century. Romanticism had a hold on these Liberals too, but the Liberals did not distort it to the extent that later-day Germans did. Even though the *Communist Manifesto* was published in 1848, the German revolution of that year was virtually unconnected with socialist thought. It was a truly Liberal revolution in the sense of 1776. But there was one flaw: anti-Semitism was already pervading the German intellectual atmosphere.

The Revolution was almost bloodless. Excitement which generated in France swept all over Europe. Reaction to Napoleonic France had been one of the driving forces of German politics for half a century. Metternich in Austria was the leading statesman of the German-speaking lands, and he spoke for absolute monarchy, repression, and reaction. When news of the February Revolution in France (which again failed to bring Liberal government to that country) reached Germany, the dike broke. Excitement flowed through all of Germany. Metternich fled almost immediately, never to return. All over Germany, Liberals, with intellectuals in the lead (as in America nearly seventy-five years before), made demands on the scores of princes who ruled them. In Berlin on March 16, several persons in an excited crowd were killed by the soldiers of Frederick William IV of Prussia. The King, extremely frightened by the incident, was forced to pay tribute to the fallen demonstrators at a mass funeral; bareheaded, he did so without demur. Royalty and commoner alike felt that the flood of Liberal sentiment was irreversible. After a couple of less important attempts by non-elected parliamentarians, an elected assembly convened at Frankfurt-am-Main in May amid wild jubilation and expectations:

> The official composition of the assembly totaled 831 representatives. . . . Of the deputies there were 4 master workers, 11 post-office officials, inspectors and the like; 46 merchants, many bankers, industrialists, and printers, and 60 landowners. In addition there were 49 university professors and teachers, 57 teachers of other schools, 157 judges and other government officials, 66 lawyers, 20 mayors, 118 higher officials, 3 diplomats, 5 librarians,

18 doctors, 33 ministers, and 43 writers—all told, 569 academi-
cians out of a total of 831 deputies. There came the leading
scholars, writers, and publicists of Germany—the historians Roh-
mer, Dahlmann, Droysen, Biedermann, Gervinus, Waitz, and
Döllinger; the political theorists Zachariä, Welcker, Robert and
Moritz von Mohl; the writers Rudolf Haym, Friedrich Theodor
Vischer, and Uhland; the patriots Jahn and Arndt; the Jewish
liberal Gabriel Riesser; the Catholic leader Bishop von Ketteler;
the radicals Blum and Ruge; the statesmen Radowitz, Römer,
Bassermann, Gagern, and Vincke. It was a most unusual galaxy
of brilliant personalities who were chosen for their individual
qualities rather than as representatives of class, group, or political
party. But they were primarily theoreticians rather than practical
politicians and statesmen; "many famous names but few political heads, very many dependent officials, few independent men
of the people" (Gutzkow).[12]

The story of that venerable body is interesting in itself, but
we need not go into it in detail here except to note its results.
It is interesting to note, however, that the representatives to that
assembly were chosen for their qualities alone. No class conflicts
were involved. This was also true of America in 1776. This ab-
sence of distinction by class is unique to the Enlightenment. Class
warfare was nearly absent in the American Revolution and very
much in evidence in the French and Russian revolutions.

(Although the French Revolution occurred during the period
of the Enlightenment, it is debatable whether the revolutionaries
who prevailed had truly accepted the Enlightenment. It may
have been the predominance of class warfare in the French Revolution which was the turning point between the growth of
democracy and the eventual rise of totalitarianism. Important
here is the concept of "a decent respect for the opinions of mankind." The degree of toleration in areas where toleration may pre-
vail without coming into direct conflict with specific revolutionary
aims can tell us much about the degree of "enlightenment" in a
revolution.)

In keeping with our practice of relating the discussion to

---

[12] Pinson, *op. cit.*, pp. 95-96.

today's America, one is struck by the intolerance exhibited by Americans today. While the Far Right is intolerant of even relatively moderate political views, beards, pot,[13] and intellectuals, the New Left is intolerant of relatively moderate political views and the non-political values of society in general—even criticizing such harmless diversions as college football. This absurdly egocentric desire of wishing that the general masses have the same values and general likes and dislikes as the most educated is only a milder form of the intolerance of the Far Right. The contrast between this contemporary lack of toleration regarding such insipid items as beards and football, and the respect for the opinions of mankind espoused by the Enlightenment, seems to be only another symptom of the unfortunate reaction against democracy in the twentieth century—a reaction which began in Eastern Europe and spread to the West through the vehicle of the world wars and a materialistic preoccupation with economic growth (as opposed to a genuine concern with poverty and related problems).

In March, 1849, the Frankfurt Assembly finally, after much debate, adopted a Liberal constitution with a monarch at the head of the government. A deputation was dispatched to Berlin to offer the crown to the King of Prussia. But the climate between the King and the Liberals had changed during the ten months of debate. The King and his court were haughty and rude to the delegation. Frederick William declined to accept the crown unless he received consent of the various German princes and sovereigns; he would not take it from mere commoners. The Revolution of 1848 in Germany was dead.

Where did the Liberals fail? Or was the failure unavoidable? No one knows, of course, but most German historians are agreed on at least one major oversight made by the Liberals. That over-

---

[13] The prohibition of non-habit-forming drugs is an exception to the death-of-puritanism thesis discussed on page 39 above. On delving into newspapers of the 1920's, one cannot help but notice the similarity between the hysterical attitudes of the drys then and of the anti-drug forces today. The principal difference seems to be that the great mass of society indulged in drinking in the 1920's while only a relatively small segment participates in the use of harmless, but illegal, drugs today. This naturally makes repeal much more difficult.

sight was the failure to take power. The Assembly made no attempt to take over the army. In an apparent naive faith in human nature, the German Liberals of '48 failed to consolidate the Revolution by physically taking over the reins of government. It was a lesson not lost on later generations of Germans.

The Liberal American Revolution, nearly seventy-five years previous, had been of a more practical nature. The Americans fought a bitter war for their revolution. By contrast, the misguided attitude of a portion of today's New Left toward power is epitomized in the phrase *flower power*, which symbolizes a retreat from power. It speaks of the power of beauty and love. It is an expression of a deep, poetical truism, but one that can be realized only by a system of government incorporating power itself and exerted by those who would "make love, not war." In the same manner that Locke's society protects man from the "state of nature" which surrounds him, a government powerful enough to guarantee man's right to be left alone by those who would foist universal military training, or any other mandatory system of labor or government service, upon him must first be developed. (Such forced government service is of course an essential characteristic of totalitarianism, including communism.) The permanent state of nuclear terror with its accompanying permanent national emergency, as well as the economic race with communism, must be stopped. What is needed is not a denial of, or dropping out from, the American Revolution but a reaffirmation of that revolution on a twentieth-century basis.

The Far Right, with their German-style, paranoic anti-communism, are no more a part of the true American Revolution than is H. Rap Brown or the militant W. E. B. DuBois Club. Rather, they represent the counterrevolution rooted in the East and in romanticism.

The concepts of flower power and dropping out are psychedelic in origin. They are curious, immature reactions to the psychedelic experience. To illustrate, let us consider the Eastern idea expressed by *yin* and *yang*. Yin is feminine. It is the period of learning. It is passiveness and childhood. Yang is the opposite. It is masculine and active. It is adulthood, parenthood, and the act of teaching. It is taking care of business and practical matters. The truly integrated person must have both yin and yang. He must be able to give as well as receive. He must learn and listen when it is required, and at other times he will find it necessary to teach and to expound. The concepts of masculine and feminine, parenthood and childhood, and all the others are never absolute, only symbolic. The individual who is striving to get there must never lose either the yin or the yang, but must be able to call on either as the situation requires. The psychedelic experience, then, is entirely yin. It is a passive period of reception and learning. When one comes down from acid, he enters a period of relative yang. His job will soon be (after some well-deserved rest) to put to work what he has learned during the experience, to get out and take care of business, if you will. Dropping out represents a state of permanent yin. Massive permanent dropping out makes it sound as if the critics of LSD are correct in maintaining that many never completely recover from a blast of acid. More likely, it may merely be mankind's inexperience with these drugs that results in massive dropping out. Not that those individuals who can afford to drop out should not have the right to do so, but generally speaking, the expression *dropping out* seems to be akin to what would have happened had Christ remained on the mount forever after achieving his psychedelic experience by fasting for forty days and creating vitamin deficiencies.

(A reasonable and, it would seem, desirable compromise would be to legalize pot and acid but to retain the illegality of the former for those under twenty-one and the latter for those under twenty-five. The reasoning for the suggestion that youths should not be permitted to take psychedelics until such an advanced age is that it is those who have not yet had time to form a philosophy who intend to drop out rather than benefit from the experience.)

Flower power represents a similar response. Most members of the New Left, except Reds and militant Negroes, merely stick their heads in the sand when it comes to power. The only practical way to achieve their desires at this juncture in history is to become involved completely in *practical* American politics; otherwise they will make the same mistake as the German Liberals in '48. They can keep their basic goals in sight if only they will drop their dogmatism. They can keep their beards and long hair and earn respect for bearded and long-haired men. There is no need to continue to accept the fiction that the American Revolution belongs to the extreme Right. It belongs to all who are willing to work within it. Those who would adopt this stance must be aggressive and defensively militant; that is, they must vote and compromise and be able to accept defeat with an English sense of fair play. But when someone tries to tell them that it is not their revolution or their country, that is the time to be prepared to fight if need be. They are not dropping out; they are being pushed out and are accepting it without resistance. Power can be realized through the ordinary democratic processes, but the counterrevolution must be defeated with force if necessary. Those who would deny moderate socialists, or any who are willing to work within the system, their rights as Americans are the enemies of 1776. It is not the other way around.

While we are on the subject of the shortcomings of the New Left, one thing that must be deplored is the attitude displayed by some of hoping that things will become worse so that they can get their way. This, of course, is dogmatism in the extreme. It is probably the worst trait of communism. Socialist revolutions are frequently justified in nations with reactionary governments and masses of impoverished people (although it must be expected that there will not be more death and suffering than is justified by the pre-revolutionary injustices). If, however, a government is making a reasonable effort to solve the problems of the people, it should be given every opportunity to continue to do so. Communists in the United States and elsewhere long for the day when conditions will become generally intolerable. This is dogmatism at its wildest. They wish for starvation, which in turn breeds violence, upon which totalitarianism is based.[14] The New Left has taken an alarming turn toward this type of thinking recently. The concept of regarding congressional liberals as the primary

---

[14] See pp. 125-28.

enemy is nothing short of dangerous. To work for the defeat of these liberals, and consequently for the advancement of the Goldwaters and the Nixons, represents a type of negative thinking that can only contribute to the death of the American Revolution; and a fascist overthrow is more likely than a communist overthrow in the nation. This declaration of war on the Morses, Fulbrights, and Hartkes has its counterpart in the civil-rights movement's drift to a virtually all-black movement. The indiscriminate anger of these blacks against *all* whites causes white backlash among latent bigots and an aloofness among the truly unprejudiced whites. The rejection of leftist politicians who are moderate enough to be elected is a commitment to totalitarianism at worst and to dictatorship at best. For any form of government other than some kind of dictatorship must be built upon the ability to compromise. Just as the Far Right created the dangerous aspects of the New Left, so in turn the dangerously dogmatic and unyielding reaction of the New Left only makes the Far Right more dangerous. If the country continues to drift into two uncompromising camps, there is absolutely no possible way that freedom can survive in America. The Left, of course, is vastly outnumbered. If the confrontation does come, the chances are extremely good that the ensuing dictatorship will be fascist.

If we do manage to pull ourselves out of this current dilemma that we seem to be in, the rightists must rid themselves of one of their habits of the past generation—that of not forgiving their political enemies. For if they are to consider perhaps millions of Americans—the entire mass of the New Left movement—as their enemies for life, the split will only be accentuated. It is this attitude by the Right that has been one of the major contributory factors in the present trend of mutual extremism.

The 1950's produced an avant-garde in the unfortunately dubbed "beat" school of literature and thought. The word *beat*, perverted by the press, was the result of a conversation between John C. Holmes (*Go, Nothing More to Declare*) and Jack Kerouac, in which Holmes thoughtfully applied the term to the generation of World War II and Korean War veterans who were appalled by the onset of the nuclear age and were searching for a solution and a sense of direction. The group that Holmes was describing are now (1967) between the ages of approximately thirty and fifty. But the philosophy was based more on *hip* than on *beat*, regardless of Holmes' casual observation. Hip is American Negro vernacular meaning "I know." According to an anthropologist friend of mine, Edward M. Buehrig, who has made a study of Negro slang back through slavery days, this is probably the original meaning of the word.[15] (We saw it bastardized in the comic strip "Freckles and His Friends" during World War II as *hep*.) Hip came to mean more. It came to be associated with the attitude surrounding the Negro revolution. One was hip who wasn't going to let Whitey walk over him. The Uncle Tom in Mississippi wasn't really hip, neither was the New York junkie, for they had permitted the white world to get them down. Hip is epitomized in the attitude of the Deacons for Defense and Justice. It had the ring of the Spirit of '76, a revolution that the Negro was joining. The term *hippie* was applied to a hip chick, and a man was a *hipster*. The hipster of the fifties was as alienated from society as the Negro. As Kerouac pointed out, what characterized this movement was a search. What they hoped to find, no one knew for sure. For many of us of that age, Hip became a reaffirmation of the American idea. We realized that our society was sick and there was little doubt that the world would be blown up some day. Any statistician could confirm that belief; he didn't need to be especially hip to make the observation. But we refused to sit back and permit it to happen without some effort to at least postpone it. Beat described the passive period of searching. Hip described the active period of emerging and trying. Beat was like taking acid. Hip is like the period after the acid scene—the indefinite period of getting straight and putting to use what has been learned. The hipster of the 1950's might have found in his travels that much of what he imagined was wrong with America was wrong with the world in general. And he might have concluded, as many did, that in order to change what was wrong with America, we must save what was good about America.

---

[15] The study resulted in an unpublished term paper.

In his recent book, *Nothing More to Declare,* Holmes pro-
claims that the work of his literary school[16] is finished, thus his title.
This essay is in direct disagreement with that conclusion. There is
a new group a half generation younger in evidence, true. One Bill
Walker used to refer to them as "junior beatniks." And the sixties'
group of flower-power hippies will always remain just that until
they begin to assert themselves within the American mainstream
of conventional politics.

If I have seemed unduly harsh with the New Left, I only
mean to shake them up a bit. Actually there are many encouraging signs that the New Left is becoming a political entity of
sorts, such as the rising tide of conscientious objection to the
draft. (For those who cannot understand why many of the same
Americans who are against the Vietnam War were very militantly
in support of Israel in the June, 1967, war, this support of such
conscientious objection may at first seem paradoxical with some
of the other positions taken in this book. For those readers, the
distinctions will become sharper as they read on. For others,
no explanation is needed.)

It does not take an especially astute observer to see other
parallels between German romantic and contemporary American
political thought. The longing for passion is evident in both. We

---

16 The beat school of the fifties produced one great poet—Allen Gins-
berg. *Howl* must go down as one of the great sociological documents of
all time. Lawrence Ferlinghetti is a very good poet. Gregory Corso is an
entertaining poet. Jack Kerouac is notable mainly because reviewers made
such a fuss about *On the Road.* Actually Holmes' *Go* is a much better and
more readable novel written in the same vein. Both fall in the realm of
entertainment and little else. In a more serious vein Thomas Pynchon's *V*
must be mentioned here, even though Pynchon is not usually associated
with that school. Ken Kesey's McMurphy, the venerable hero of *One Flew
Over the Cuckoo's Nest,* is the essence of hip. The novel is one of the few
great ones to come out of the postwar generation of American writers.
Another is Joseph Heller's hilarious *Catch-22.* Norman Mailer is very good
in high spots and more subtle than some. James Baldwin articulately presents the position of the American Negro. Although he says little which is
original, his better work is a good primer for white bigots. All these men
can be correctly associated with the Hip school of the postwar years.

have seen that Germany was not without her Liberals. Among intellectuals they were in the majority by 1848. But the failure of the Liberals to act in a positive manner at the Frankfurt Assembly doomed the revolution of 1848–49, just as the failure of American radicals to modify their views and work within the framework of the ready-made American Revolution seems to doom their efforts, if we may call them that, for a "Democratic Society." The passion of youth is evident on both right and left. But it is on the right that extreme passion presents the greatest menace. For when the nuclear generation came of age, reaction was already respectable. There were reactionaries in government, including Congress, and partly because of the anti-communism of the forties and fifties their leftist counterparts were few and held no positions of influence.

The contemporary youth of America, in a virtual panic and with each side having its own peculiar formula for saving the world, are failing to reach any agreement in the center. Radicals are denying themselves the American Revolution and reactionaries are perverting it. Thus, among today's educated youth there is only a small group of moderates who are willing to seek solutions through compromise and reason. And compromise is the essence of democracy. In fact, if the segments of a society find themselves unable to reason together, by definition some form of dictatorship must evolve. At best the present trends can lead us to a Latin-American type of dictatorship of the milder, benevolent form. At worst, of course, it can lead us to totalitarianism. Attempts to blow up the Statue of Liberty and the Washington Monument, for instance, are all too similar to acts in countries where an unworkable inability to achieve any semblance of democracy has long been demonstrated. If both, rather than one, of the groups of extremists were politically powerful today in America—and power is the key which leftists are denying themselves—then the policies of this country, if democracy could be maintained, would swing so widely from one administration to another that chaos might result.

It is of course the Right that is so similar to Father Jahn in philosophy. Certainly the Young Republicans, who embody ex-

tremism to a greater extent than the Republican National Committee, succeeded in nominating their candidate in 1964; they show
no sign of modifying their views and are full of Jahn-like passion. Friedrich von Schlegel invited Germany to remember her
spiritual mission; the Right calls upon America to remember
hers. Germany sought her identity in the glorious days of the
barbaric conquests of Rome and the rest of Europe; America
seeks hers, in the eyes of the Far Right, in the glorious nineteenth-
century days of the conquest of the frontier, Mexico, and the
American Indian. Europe, except for Germany, was decadent;
the world, except for America and an occasional exception or two,
such as Canada, is overrun with decadent socialism. Schlegel
felt that the nation was the highest unity attainable; and in spite
of their disdain of big government, our reactionaries seem to find
in this nation the highest unity attainable. They exhort a crude
style of patriotism while proposing that we leave the UN or refuse to trade with Rumania. Germany was to be based upon blood
and language; too many of our Far Rightists (there are some
notable exceptions) are racial and even religious bigots. At times
it seems the only thing they have retained of our Western heritage
is a love for capitalism.

More alarming is the fact that we have progressed to the stage
of Father Jahn's war against the West. New organizations such as
the Minutemen and the Counter Insurgency Council on the right,
and the Harlem Mau Maus on the left, are forever springing up.
In no way can such organizations be interpreted as being a part
of our Western heritage. (It should be pointed out here that the
Deacons for Defense and Justice, which started in Louisiana
and is *not* aggressive but is rather defensive in nature, is in no
way similar in philosophy to the above-mentioned groups.) The
militant and armed reactionary groups are Eastern in philosophy
and outlook (frequently unbeknownst to themselves) and just
as dangerous to the Western way of life as communism would be
if it were widespread in this country:

> ... Most important was his [Jahn's] influence on three move-
> ments which were not only characteristic of German nationalism
> but models as well for similar trends in central and eastern Eu-

rope: free corps of patriotic volunteers . . . associations for the
training of patriotic fighters; and . . . fraternities aflame with
nationalistic zeal.[17]

As for the Young Republicans, their appeal is easily understood. It is a rather natural thing for one to be influenced by
childhood environment. Youth always has tended to be somewhat
extreme, and with the realities of the nuclear age that tendency
has become greatly exaggerated. The extreme position closest to
the childhood political environment of most Americans is this
reactionary position. Such a position, of course, represents a
generally unsophisticated view. (Most young right-wing extremists who change to a moderate viewpoint probably do so in their
early twenties. It would seem, then, that if this were true, the
voting age should be raised to twenty-five instead of lowered to
eighteen or nineteen, as is the present trend.)

On the other extreme, currently exemplified to a certain
extent by some of the New Left and to a greater extent by communism, is a group of youths whose political position stems partially from rebellion for its sake alone, rather than from a cool,
pragmatic approach. This group is just as immature as the Far
Right. Radicalism and even reaction are not always undesirable:
the desirability depends always upon the conditions existing in
the country in question. Circumstances must, however, be extreme
to justify the use of violence; all other reasonable alternatives
should be tried first. An indication of one's political maturity is
whether or not he will deviate from dogma on a reasonable number of issues. For instance, suppose an apparently liberal American took a stand against fluoridation of public water supplies.[18]
This would lead one to suspect that at least some of his positions
had been logically thought out, no matter how irrational the
conclusion might appear on the surface. Socialism in this country

---

[17] Kohn, *op. cit.*, pp. 82-83. The reader might find it interesting to substitute the words *American* and *black* for *German* in this quotation.

[18] Fluoridation can be scientifically and reasonably opposed upon the
ground that a generation of testing is needed to ascertain whether it is
completely safe with regard to side effects—hardening of the arteries, for
example. Unfortunately the irrational grounds upon which it has been
opposed have obscured scientific perspective.

is not necessarily the result of immature thinking, although it often is when it denotes a concern over the ownership of property rather than the use of property. Dogmatism, socialistic or otherwise, can also be a block to positive compromise and progress. A notable case in point is the record of land reform in many Latin-American countries and recently in Egypt. Many of these attempts were unsuccessful in their professed goals and only made matters worse because the governments involved confused control of ownership with control of land use.

We will now break with chronology in our historical narrative in order to trace the economic story of the past two centuries without interruption. We will then return to a political discussion beginning again with Germany and the pre-World War I period and finally bring economic and political history together with our discussion of the twentieth century, focused principally upon the United States. I will continue to comment upon the historical narrative as seems appropriate in order to forward this moderate viewpoint. We will first turn to England and jump back a bit to look at the much maligned Manchester school of economics.

The Manchester school of economics is the classical school of Adam Smith, David Ricardo, and laissez faire. It is presumed that most readers are generally familiar with the ideas produced by the classical economists. Laissez faire is, of course, the concept upon which our conservatives and reactionaries of today base their idea of "the least government the better" with regard to industry and commerce. It was the economic philosophy of the classical Liberals who were reacting to the inefficient government controls of mercantilism. Smith's *Wealth of Nations,* in which he expounded this doctrine, was published, coincidentally, in 1776.

When carried to an international scale (macrocosm), laissez faire requires the abolishment of tariff barriers. This was virtually achieved in Britain in 1846, and free trade predominated in Britain until the early years of the twentieth century, when the British Empire became a sort of trade union. Free trade no doubt works to the advantage of nearly all countries involved when free flow of labor, capital, and foreign exchange is permitted to offset any imbalances. It does, of course, usually require reciprocity. Britain was able to follow a free-trade policy without reciprocity by most other nations because of her consistently favorable balance of payments. When she began to lose her ability to maintain a favorable balance of payments in conjunction with her policy of unilateral free trade, she was forced to re-establish a tariff policy. (Perhaps a more reasonable basis than reciprocity for the establishment of tariffs would be to set tariffs on virtually all goods, with exceptions for scarce foodstuffs or war materiel when necessary, at the amount the ratio of imports to exports exceeded one the previous year, adjusted for the existing tariff; as the ratio decreased so would the tariff and vice versa.)

Laissez faire exhibited imperfections domestically as well. The Industrial Revolution found laborers crowded together in cities in unsanitary conditions and living on mere subsistence wages (and occasionally less). Hours were long, and women and children often worked under conditions that would be considered intolerable today. Alcoholism, as an escape from such squalor, became a serious problem; the condition of the worker was generally dismal. Whether or not his condition was worse than before he left the countryside is an academic question. Most historians today believe that the reform movements that resulted were due to an increase in social awareness resulting from concentration of the impoverished population in cities rather than a general worsening of the workers' conditions. In any event, laissez faire did not solve the problem, even though a few industrialists displayed admirable humanitarian traits by providing decent wages and working conditions on their own initiative. Economics became known as "the dismal science" when Thomas Malthus wrote his probably valid but premature essay on population for the *Encyclopaedia Britannica,* and Ricardo propounded his invalid "iron law of wages," which claimed that the laborer was always bound to live only on a subsistence level.

In the United States "trusts" became a serious problem. The railroads showed a cynical lack of consideration for the public interest in their manipulation of rates and land. Financial institutions, food processors, and mining interests all abused the

privileges bestowed upon them by the system. The reform movement which arose produced some notable literature around the
turn of the century. Upton Sinclair's novels 'are rather tiring
bits of socialist propaganda and are interesting today mainly as
period pieces, but Frank Norris's *The Octopus* is an excellent
extravaganza in which the villain is the Southern Pacific Railroad.
Norris's book is a good example of the transition in American literature from romanticism to twentieth-century realism, containing
elements of both. The Interstate Commerce Act of 1887 and the
Clayton Anti-Trust Act of 1914—infringements on pure laissez
faire—improved the situation immensely. It might be interesting
for the reader to speculate for a moment whether there is some
quality in the American character that made such antitrust legislation necessary, while many other industrial nations have not
felt the necessity to pass such legislation. Laws to improve the
position of labor are, however, generally universal.

The twentieth century brought with it three great events:
World War I, the worldwide depression of the 1930's, and World
War II. World War I brought on an especially profound change
in the socio-economic structure of Europe and America. A quote
from Palmer and Colton will help us to understand the tremendous impact that that war had upon twentieth-century society;

> European society was forced by the First World War into
> many basic changes that were to prove more lasting than the
> war itself. First of all, the war profoundly affected capitalism as
> previously known. Essential to the older capitalism (or economic
> liberalism, or free private enterprise) had been the idea that
> government should leave business alone, or at the most regulate
> certain general conditions under which business men went about
> their affairs. Before 1914 governments had increasingly come into
> the economic field. They had put up tariffs, protected national
> industries, sought for markets or raw materials by imperialist
> expansion, or passed protective social legislation to benefit the
> wage-earning classes. During the war all belligerent governments
> controlled the economic system far more minutely. Indeed, the
> idea of the "planned economy" was first applied in the First
> World War. For the first time (with such rare and archaic prece-

dents as the French dictatorship of 1793) the state attempted
to direct all the wealth, resources and moral purpose of society
to a single end.

. . . By 1916 each government had set up a system of boards,
bureaus, councils and commissions to coordinate its war effort.
The aim was to see that all manpower was effectively utilized, and
that all natural resources within the country, and all that could
possibly be imported, were employed where they would do
the most good. In the stress of war free competition was found
to be wasteful and undirected private enterprise too uncertain
and too slow. The profit motive came into disrepute. Those who
exploited shortages to make big profits were stigmatized as
"profiteers." Production for civilian use, or for mere luxury purposes, was cut to a minimum. Businessmen were not allowed
to set up or close down factories as they chose. It was impossible
to start a new business without government approval, because
the flotation of stocks and bonds was controlled, and raw mate-
rials were made available only as the government wished. It was
equally impossible to shut down a business engaged in war production; if a factory was inefficient or unprofitable the government
kept it going anyway, making up the losses, so that in some cases
management came to expect government support. Here too the
tests of competition and profitableness were abandoned. The
new goal was coordination or "rationalization" of production in
the interests of the country as a whole . . . For the upper and
middle classes it became embarrassing to show their comforts too
openly. It was patriotic to eat meagerly and to wear old clothes.
War gave a new impetus even to the idea of economic equality,
if only to enlist rich and poor alike in a common cause.

Military conscription was the first step in the allocation of
manpower. Draft boards told some men to report to the army,
granting exemption to others to work safely in war industries.
Given the casualty rates at the front, state determination over
individual life could hardly go farther. With the insatiable need
for troops, drawing in men originally exempted or at first rejected
as physically inadequate, great numbers of women poured into
factories and offices, and in Britain even into newly organized
women's branches of the armed forces. Women took over many
jobs which it had been thought only men could do. Since their
invasion proved to be permanent, the labor force of all countries

was enlarged, women's place in society was revolutionized, the institution of marriage and the relations of husband and wife were transformed, and the lives, liberty, and outlook of millions of individual women were turned outwards from the home . . . by influencing wage scales, granting draft exemptions, forcing some industries to expand, and others to contract or stand still, and propagandizing the idea that work in an arms factory was patriotic, the state shifted vast numbers of workers to war production. . . .

Governments controlled all foreign trade. It was intolerable to let private citizens ship off the country's resources at their own whim. It was equally intolerable to let them use up foreign exchange by importing unneeded goods, or to drive up prices of necessities by competing with one another. Foreign trade became a state monopoly, in which private firms operated under strict licenses and quotas. . . .

All the belligerent governments during the war attempted to control ideas as they did economic production. Freedom of thought, respected everywhere in Europe for half a century, went into the discard. Propaganda and censorship became more effective than any government, however despotic, had ever been able to devise. No one was allowed to sow doubt by raising any basic questions.

. . . Placards, posters, diplomatic white papers, schoolbooks, public lectures, solemn editorials, and slanted news reports conveyed the message. The new universal literacy, the mass press, the new moving pictures, proved to be ideal media for the direction of popular thinking. Intellectuals and professors advanced complicated reasons, usually historical, for loathing and crushing the enemy. In Allied countries the Kaiser was portrayed as a demon, with glaring eyes and abnormally bristling mustaches, bent on the mad project of conquest of the world. In Germany people were taught to dread the day when Cossacks and Senegalese Negroes should rape German women, and to hate England as the inveterate enemy which inhumanly starved little children with its blockade. Each side convinced itself that all right was on its side, and all wrong, wickedness, and barbarity on the other. An inflamed opinion helped to sustain men and women in such a fearsome struggle. But when it came time to make peace the rooted convictions, fixed ideas, profound aversions, hates, and fears became an obstacle to political judgment.[19]

These war societies not only provided the seeds for totalitarianm, they seriously brought into question the validity of laissez aire, and with it Liberalism, as a viable twentieth-century doc-ine. Because of Britain's change from a creditor to a debtor untry, which emphasized the fact that free trade was no longer asible for her; because of the great economic and social changes at took place in European society as a result of the world ars; and because of the Great Depression of the 1930's, it was lt in some quarters that Liberalism and the Enlightenment were ead.

Actually there was no reason for such a pessimistic view of uropean society. None of the great ideas of Locke, Jefferson, nd Wilson were dying on their own. But the world had changed, nd a pragmatic reappraisal was needed. What brought on the ternational monetary crisis causing the worldwide depression the 1930's? In view of changing conditions, what part of the ar economies should or must be kept? Since a great physical ange in the structure of European society had occurred, what as necessary to ensure that the good was not thrown out with e bad? These were the questions to be answered by those in fluential positions at the time. To discard all the existing values nd institutions of Western European society was *not* the answer. opefully we could improve our society and economic system ithin the existing structure and retain our Western personality. or, to borrow a bit from the romanticism which we have harshly riticized, a people should strive to develop its own personality ithin reasonable bounds. The totalitarianism that arose in East-rn and Central Europe, with its stress on the state rather than e individual, could not serve this purpose for the West. We eeded to retain our freedoms—to remain Western.

In the area of commerce the Western peoples also wanted reedom. Our problem was to retain commercial freedom as

---

[19] *Op. cit.*, pp. 689-91, 693-94.

much as possible while at the same time adjusting to the new er.
and protecting the public welfare. The philosopher for this was
naturally enough, John Locke: ". . . As much as any one can make
use of to any advantage of life before it spoils, so much he may
by his labour fix a property in. Whatever is beyond this is more
than his share, and belongs to others. . . ."[20] This laid the ground
for compromise in the area of property. The long-accepted doc
trine of public utility is consistent with Locke. Let us here define
the *public* as being generally synonymous with the *consumer*
This is obvious if one thinks about it, for herein lies one of the
few economic functions that every individual in every society
performs: he consumes goods and services and exchanges hi
money for them. If the reader will allow me to express opinion
at this juncture, the government should naturally have the righ
to protect the consumer (public) from the abuses which the
trusts foisted upon the public in the late nineteenth century
(Too many such abuses still exist because of the reluctance of
Congress to set up a Department of the Consumer, and pass legis
lation regarding packaging, misleading advertising, quotation
of interest rates, and the like.) The government needs the righ
to take action in behalf of the consumer which is necessary to
protect his interests. This is as basic as taking legal action or
"behalf of the people of the State of California" in a crimina
case. The government must represent the consumer and hence the
national interest in both tort and criminal cases with regard to
business and industry. The doctrine of public utility can be
extended to include nationalization of railroads and communica
tions—provided proper payment is made to the former owners
On the other hand, if power is in danger of being misused and
that power is due to a concentration of wealth, then the tax base
can be adjusted as a remedial measure. The government must be
careful not to become involved in class warfare. If the proponent
of redistributing the wealth propose a basic change in the tax
base, it should be demonstrated by them that their proposed
change will provide enough additional revenue to enable the
government to alleviate poverty substantially at the lower end o.

---

[20] *Op. cit.,* pp 353-56.

he economic scale, prevent the gross misuse of wealth, or serve
ome other important function. (It is questionable whether our pro-
;ressive income-tax and inheritance-tax systems are a budgetary
necessity. The percentage of the national budget supported by the
uppermost economic strata is relatively quite small. These taxes
do, however, serve to keep wealth from becoming too concen-
rated and possibly misused, either economically or politically;
or this reason they are defensible.) Our concern here is not to
amper with the freedoms of the wealthy, for society certainly
has a surplus of people and need not worry about each individual's contribution to it. That is and should be the concern
of the individual himself. If we are to accept the basic Western
idea that the individual citizen is of primary importance instead
f the concept that the nation is foremost, then every individual,
barring extreme and temporary national emergency, must decide
ow much he needs to feel he is contributing to society in order
o satisfy his individual self. For the state to dictate just how much
nd what each individual should do in order to be happy is of
ourse impossible and an infringement upon the individual's right
o the pursuit of *his* happiness, whether he be idly rich or a hippie.

Here we have the whole heart of the counterrevolution in this
ountry—not with regard to economics in particular but with re-
ard to life in general. The lack of respect for individual freedom
s by no means confined to the Left but is found throughout
American society.

Author's Note: To attempt to explain the monetary collapse
f 1929 ff., we will examine the Vietnam monetary crisis as it was
n 1967. As this book goes to press, the economic situation has
hanged substantially. We are far from out of the storm described
elow, but two major monetary events have occurred recently
which foster hope. First was the exceptionally strong buying on
record volume in April, 1968, on the New York Stock Exchange
nmediately after President Johnson's now famous March 31
peech. At that time the market appeared to be about two weeks
way from a major panic. The 1929–32 bear market ended on a
igh-volume rally of the same nature. It seems likely that the

President, who apparently became suddenly aware of the serious ness of the Vietnam monetary crisis during the money crunc of October, 1966, may have been deeply influenced by th delicate position of the market when he decided to back down i Vietnam. His great act of humility (see page 21), which seem sincere enough at this writing, came just in time. The second even was the immense loan to Great Britain to support the pound. Th loan, announced on July 15, 1968, three days prior to this writing also came at the very last minute. I quote from *The Internatione Harry Schultz Letter* of July 1, 1968. Mr. Schultz writes *the* leac ing financial letter on the international money markets, sponsor monetary seminars for leaders in the world of finance, and su cessfully handles portfolios of enormous sums. I have spelled o Schultz' abbreviations. The letter was written two weeks befor the loan was announced:

Sterling is in big trouble. Here in London the cautious whispers among the in-people amount to: "The pound can't last through the summer." US subscribers will watch with all-out attention, for *this* time whither the pound goeth, so goeth the US dollar. And with the dollar will fall most currencies of the world (in varying degrees), exempting perhaps only the Swiss franc and the mark. Just how bad is it? Here's a cross section of facts: Dr. Franz Aschinger, economic counselor to the Swiss Bank Corp. (one of the big three [Swiss banks]) says, "The view now largely held by central banks is that aid to Great Britain has reached its ultimate *limits*. Further credits for Great Britain's balance of payments are neither discussable, recommended, advisable or possible." How much louder can you say NO than that? He added, "The international monetary scene is made gloomy today by the fact that the pound, in spite of 14% devaluation seven months ago, is still in the same difficulty." The Bank of England (and I quote a London paper) "is virtually broke for the first time in Great Britain's long history." Almost every day last week the pound thumped to new all-time lows. . . .

Some readers will ask, "But Dr. Aschinger has turned out to b 'wrong' even before this book goes to press. Why print such state ments?" Such a reaction misses the point, which is how sick th monetary situation of the Western countries was and still is; f when a currency in that situation is supported by such a massive loan, the Western nations are indeed in panic. By the same token, the main part of this book was written in the summer of 1967 and this note in July, 1968. Since this is not a market letter but a political essay, there seems no better way to illustrate the monetary lunacy of Vietnam nor to strengthen the theory discussed below—that imperialism and capitalism are no longer related—than to describe the situation as it appeared in 1967. I have been advised by some friends outside the world of finance to update the following discussion, for it seems that now there is a ray or two of economic hope. This too would miss the whole point. Johnson's March 31, 1968, speech took the financial world by as much surprise as it did the rest of the population. Those who last any length of time in the world of finance know that the secret to success is to admit quickly and without vanity when they are in error. It is with this attitude that the following assessment of the situation a year ago is freely published now. Even though there may now be some chance to avoid the worst, the discussion is offered for historical perspective.

Our worries about this problem are by no means over, but at this time we have some breathing space. The stock market is currently in good technical condition, and it is difficult to see how it could crash for a couple of months from this writing no matter what happened. But it has not yet told us whether the first market day after President Johnson's March 31 speech was the start of a new bull market or an enormous bull trap. Another strong rally on even higher volume than the April rally would indicate that the market is indeed out of danger. There is a tremendously high-volume, bull-bear fight taking place at this writing (and has been since early May) with high buying pressures against the resistance area which represents the largest (three-year) sell-off in history. If this resistance area were strongly penetrated, it would not be a classical Dow theory bull market signal, but it should convince all but the most stubborn bears. Yet there is still at least one major technical indicator (which need not be described here except to say that it is an indicator of good versus bad buying, or "speculation") which is still hitting all-time thirty-

year lows. And the dollar, which is now supporting the pound, i
no longer a strong currency due to the United States balance o
payments problem. Troubles are bound to result from the crisi
even if everything goes as smoothly as possible from now on—
inflation and government austerity programs, for example. But i»
any event there is now some hope. Perhaps if everything goe
perfectly for a year or so, gold *can* actually be demonetized afte
all. As for the arguments of those who maintain that we hav«
"built-in safeguards" today that we didn't have in the 1930's, the⟩
are only partially correct. Every built-in safeguard in the world
whether it be in economics or auto safety, has its limitations, es
pecially when abused. Furthermore, if the United States continue
to foster wars for which she is unwilling to pay, new monetar⟩
crises are bound to arise even if we somehow manage to get ou
of this one. And many of those "built-in safeguards" have alread⟩
been used.

At the present there appears to be a very definite danger tha»
the economy may completely collapse sometime between now an‹
the early 1970's as a result of what has already transpired, whethe
peace comes or not. An economy as big as ours does not collaps‹
overnight. If the general public were to misinterpret such a⟩
event, blaming it upon peace or a cutback in general spending
for example, the results could be tragic.

If the crisis is indeed being halted, it is a monumental achieve
ment, for it would mark the first time in world economic histor⟩
that the processes of major liquidation had been successfully re
versed once they were set in motion. In any event it will pay u
to contemplate for a moment what we may narrowly have misse‹
and why.

Note: Much, but certainly not all, of the discussion for th
next several pages is highly technical. The average reader wil
want to skim over the technical details, searching for the non
technical parts. None of the conclusions will be missed in thi
manner—only the evidence. For the serious stock-market student
the section is more easily followed when read in conjunction witl
a long-term chart of the Dow-Jones Industrial Average, prefer
ably going back to around 1924 and complete with trading vol

ume. A more detailed chart of the market averages on a weekly basis from 1965 onward is also interesting. Such charts may be found in most brokerage firms and in good business libraries.

To attempt to answer the question we brought up a few pages earlier as to what actually happened to the monetary systems of the nations in 1929, we will examine the stock market as it stands in the summer of 1967.

At the time this page is being written (July 20, 1967) the Dow-Jones Industrial Average stands at about 910 and the Standard and Poor's Index of 500 stocks stands near its all-time high. A book in the social sciences, written at such a time, runs the risk of being obsolete by the time it sees print. The cold-war boom is making its last gasps. At this point there is no way of telling where the bear market will finally bottom out nor how long a depression should last. This is being written without knowing whether the panic will entail a severe crash, how many bank failures there will be, what devaluations in the world currencies will have to be made, or how long it will take for the panicked country to end the Vietnam War. But whatever happens, loud voices will be raised against the "system," Wall Street, the President, Congress, and virtually every aspect of American life. Some of these criticisms will be correct, but most will only cloud the real issues. We will again run the risk, when the inevitable changes are made, of discarding more good than bad. Our problem is to find out exactly what caused the current panic in order to work on its causes. If we change only the symptoms, no gain will ensue. If we are to legislate wisely, we must understand the causes of the massive economic problems we seem about to encounter.

Economic historians have traditionally listed three types of panics: gold panics, credit panics, and combination panics (simply a combination of the first two). Actually, a gold panic and a credit panic are essentially the same phenomenon, the three distinctions describing only the money basis of the nation in panic. Gold panics were caused when the supply of a nation's gold became depleted to such a state that it was felt the government was in serious danger of being unable to meet its obligations. If this became a reality, the currency would have to be devalued in terms of gold. If there was an open gold market, people would buy gold; foreign creditors would demand gold instead of dollars or francs, and the panic would snowball. When normal times resumed, those who had been early enough in the rush to get out of currency and investments could safely sell their gold and resume normal operations, and the gold would begin to flow back into government coffers. When the gold standard was eliminated, more pressure was put upon credit, and the possibility of pure credit panics was increased. Whatever shortcomings the gold standard may have had and however arbitrary the selection of gold as a monetary base may seem, the gold standard did provide an easily understood, simple balance sheet for government treasuries. Presidents, congressmen, premiers, and members of parliaments are less likely to foresee an oncoming credit panic than a developing gold panic; and with a credit base they are even more likely to eventually extend their government's credit to the point of no return simply because analysis of the money markets becomes more complex when gold is removed as a stabilizer. There seems to be no logical reason why a socialist government would not be just as susceptible to a panic as the government of a country with a capitalistic system. The causes of such panics today are virtually always found in the government of the nation in panic or in the government of a mighty nation with which the panicked nation is closely associated.

To understand the current situation, we must go back to 1965. The Vietnam Bear Market technically started in that year. Students of the bond markets can, in normal times, predict the ups and downs of the stock market to some extent. One method for doing this is to watch bond yields. When yields on low-grade bonds go up relative to yields on higher-grade bonds, this is an indication of less confidence in the economy, for it means that the big, stabilizing money is taking its money out of the riskier investment (low-grade bonds) and putting it into safer high-grade bonds. (Bond prices change inversely to their yields; to say that yields are rising is merely another way of saying that bonds are falling.) It follows that when the stabilizing money flows from riskier low-grade bonds, it will also forsake an even riskier investment—the stock market. When the opposite situation develops between high- and low-grade bond yields, the money flows back into stocks, and the stock market will normally advance. This seemingly complicated formula is easily plotted with a device known as Barron's Confidence Index, which is exactly that—a ratio of yields on low-grade to high-grade bonds. (The trick in using the Confidence Index for personal gain is in being able to correlate the points in the Confidence Index with those in the Dow-Jones Industrial Average at the time that the stock market is changing direction, also taking into consideration the fact that the Confidence Index does not tell us how far or how fast the stock market will move but only in which direction. One can easily get caught selling short, for instance, on the strength of a fairly sharp downward dip in the CI, which turns out to be only a slow, downward drift in the Dow.) This Confidence Index was started by *Barron's* in 1932 and has worked more or less perfectly until 1966, although its value to stock-market analysis wasn't realized until the 1950's. The apparent reason that the market doesn't rise or fall at the same time as the CI, but follows instead in a few weeks, is that the general public, as well as lesser institutions whose funds finally can no longer hold prices without the more stable money, keep the prevailing trend continuing for a while. With the hundreds of millions and sometimes billions of dollars of big money providing upward or downward pressures, even the United States government with its entire national budget, if we hypothetically allowed the Treasury to play the stock market, could not forestall a major downslide for long once the confidence of the financial world had been severely shaken. Individual investors acting on news or incorrect psychology can only cause minor fluctuations in the stock market. Rises and falls of even intermediate proportions (three weeks or more) are never caused by stock traders. Thus cries against "speculation" being the cause of a stock-market crash are sheer nonsense. The stock market, because of its more highly developed averages and charts, is merely the most graphic picture we have of a money system functioning normally and occasionally falling apart, usually because of governmental irresponsibility. (How many remember the bond-market crash in the last major bear market?) If Mrs. Smith bought stock at Dow 1,000, that is unfortunate. But to blame Mrs. Smith and her kith and kin is simply not coping with the problem.

In 1965 President Johnson accelerated the Vietnam War. This is the very root of the current trouble in the money markets. We simply could not afford such an effort without a great austerity program similar to that of the world wars. Liberals had been forwarding the Keynesian theory that deficit spending could be a useful tool in stimulating a sluggish economy. Conservatives strenuously objected. Both were absolutely correct in moderation and ridiculous in the extreme. Keynes maintained that budget surpluses should be used to build up the treasury in boom times so that the government could afford the periods of depression. Especially after 1950 the government embarked upon a policy of accepting no lows at all in the economy. At the first sign of even a much needed minor recession, the pump would be primed with funds. After the "danger" was over, the economy would embark upon its steep and dangerous ascent. There was virtually no sincere attempt whatever to put Keynesian theory to work by cutting spending and increasing taxes as the upward rush to the top continued. We told ourselves that there was an "economic race" with the communistic world. Hurry, they're only fifty years behind! Good God, they're growing faster! This was the Great Cold War Bull Market—three times as massive as the Coolidge boom. Then along came LBJ, unsophisticated in matters of economics. He looked back upon thirty years of growth which had been, to a large extent, one-sided Keynesian in nature. But no one had yet gone quite so far in extending the government's credit as his administration was about to do.

The technical beginning of the Vietnam Bear Market was in May, 1965. The financial world was beginning to doubt the fiscal soundness of the tremendous expenditure involved in the Vietnam adventure. The advance-decline line, which is the real measurement of the stock market, topped out at that time, never to return

nor even seriously approach that all-time high. (The advance-
decline line is a running total of the number of stocks advancing
daily minus the number declining.) The decline which started
in May, 1965, took the Dow from 940 to 840. After rising above
its old top of 940 without advance-decline confirmation, as it
rebounded from the June low, the Dow made a formation on
extremely high volume much like the "shelf" in the first six
months of 1929. Our shelf is harder to see since it is only a three-
month formation. (The appearance of the shelf before Hoover
took office in March, 1929, incidentally, would seem to indicate
that Coolidge, not Hoover, was in office when the panic began.
There is a beginning of a high volume sell-off indicative of crash
formations in the latter part of the Coolidge administration. Such
volume always signals a major top or bottom. Hoover can be
criticized for not concerning himself more with emergency legislation, but it seems that to blame his administration for causing
the panic, and therefore the depression, is to misplace the blame.)

The 100-point drop in May–June of '65 was well signaled by
the Confidence Index in advance. It was already under way when
Federal Reserve Board Chairman William McChesney Martin
warned against speculation and economic excesses and compared
the situation with that of 1929. The day of his speech the market
took a fairly large drop and the entire decline was labeled "the
Martin decline" by those who did not understand the money
markets. By the same token Roger Babson had made a speech
on September 5, 1929, warning against the crash that would come
"sooner or later." A market dip ensued, and it was immediately
labeled "the Babson break." What was not considered by those
who so labeled it is that Babson, whose opinion was not particularly respected by the financial world in general, had made similar
public statements before and the market had not reacted.[21]

The stock market rebounded from the May–June decline of
1965 with verve. But by early September the first obvious
danger signal was beginning to develop. As the market passed
the area of 940 on the way up, volume increased to a rate not

---

[21] John Kenneth Galbraith, *The Great Crash, 1929* (Boston: Houghton
Mifflin, 1948), pp. 89-90.

seen since the last major bear market. The big money was
getting out at the top. In February, 1966, the Dow closed at
995. Now a second major indicator was seeing its top. And
ominously the advance-decline line had not come close to equal-
ing its previous May, 1965, top. From that point, the market
went into an eight-month decline, bottoming out at 744. On the
way down, volume, although still high, noticeably slackened after
passing a consolidation at approximately the same point it had
increased on the way up—the middle 900's. And the volume at
the very bottom, on the day the Dow closed at 744 and turned
around, wasn't nearly as heavy as in the several weeks near the
top when the big money was unloading. This relatively light
volume at this point was another serious danger signal. It meant
that the final bottom had probably not yet been reached.

Just before the market reached that bottom, something interesting happened to the Confidence Index. It dropped sharply
and then shot up even more steeply (in July and August, 1966)
in a spectacular rise to unprecedented heights, indicating almost no difference in bond yields. Followers of the CI immediately turned bullish, until in September they read an article by
Granville in *Barron's*. Granville, who is the recognized authority
on the CI, stated that this particular rise, unprecedented in its
sharpness, did not represent the normal flow of money within
the bond market. He felt that for the first time since the index's
inception in 1932 it was not working properly. By analyzing
interest rates themselves, he concluded that the rise in the CI
represented the bond market in a "full scale rout." Investors
were not putting their money into lower-grade bonds but were
fleeing the bond market entirely. As demand for all bonds
approached zero, the high-grade bonds approached the same
interest rate as low-grade bonds and the CI consequently approached 100. Rather than being a sign of high confidence, the
spectacular rise in the CI represented "no confidence at all."[22]

As this is being written, the rebound from the first leg of the

---

[22] Joseph E. Granville, "Vote of No Confidence," *Barron's*, Sept. 12,
1966, pp. 3, 10.

bear market which began in 1966 is nearly over. This baby bull market was extremely strong in buying pressures early in 1967, but is now so technically weak that it could fall apart at any time. Yesterday alone (July 19) about a half billion dollars' worth of stock changed hands on the New York Stock Exchange, most of it essentially in the manner in which it changes hands at all bull-market tops. It is an awe-inspiring thing to watch.

Looking at the long-term chart, it appears that the bear market is going to be immense. The Johnson administration is responsible for the immediate causes of the panic. The reasons for the severity of the decline and the potential depression go back at least to the Eisenhower years. The policy of maintaining only upward fluctuations in the business cycle could only end in disaster. Panics occur at relatively frequent intervals and it may be too much to expect mere human leadership to avoid them entirely. If, however, a solid, gradual rate of growth over the decades with *both* ups and downs were accepted as part of the general policy of government, major bear markets could probably be avoided. To illustrate, we will again turn to the stock market. In the period from 1914 to 1924, the market fluctuated between approximately Dow 53 and Dow 120. This is a sizable fluctuation in percentages, to be sure, but ups and downs are rather orderly. In December, 1924, the previous high was broken and a precipitous advance was in high gear by 1927. All in all a nearly uninterrupted rise of 320 per cent was achieved in five years. There was then no chart support for a long way. The first time the market turned about it was bound to crash and to pick up impetus as it moved along. If any lesson was to be garnered from 1929, it should have been this. The impetus of the 1929–32 major bear market was so great that the market continued on down to 41 in spite of the major support, around 100, from pre-1924 days. This was verified by the fact that when a bona fide upside breakout from the normal channel (a channel that, when drawn in on a long-term chart, encloses all fluctuations of the Dow-Jones Industrial Average for at least the last fifty-five years *except* the Coolidge Boom and the Great Cold War Bull Market) was finally made in 1933 to definitely end the bear market, it immediately went back up to a level of 100. From 1933 to 1950 the market made rather moderate ups and downs again. Sudden drops in 1937, 1940, and 1946 turned out to be rather moderate and represented *minor* bear markets, because firm economic building had been done with fluctuations on both side of the business cycle, and previous support levels, built by preceding consolidations, braked the decline.

In 1950 an important high was broken, and by 1954 the climb had become too steep again. From the high of about 520 in 1956 back down to the 1953 low in the middle 250's was a drop of over 50 per cent, and no other support existed. The Eisenhower administration stepped into an economy that had already been permitted to rise too fast, and with a strong effort avoided a "recession"; the market immediately resumed its steep climb, unfortunately postponing the day of reckoning. The fact that volume did not look anything like 1929 in showing the great distribution of a major bear market indicated that the adjustment would still have been safe regarding the preservation of national and world economies. Even the Kennedy bear market of 1961–62 could not have developed into a true major bear market, as is seen by studying volume, although it would certainly have hurt had it not been nipped in the bud. The Vietnam Bear Market, which it should properly be called, contains a phenomenon absent in 1929—a double volume blowoff, the first part in late 1965 and early 1966, the second in the first few months of 1967. This is because no real attempt was made to solve the basic problem on the rebound—the high-deficit war spending. Between 1949 and 1966 the market made a steep ascent of about 525 per cent. After the climb became dangerously steep—Eisenhower's unheeded danger signal—the "Cold War Bull Market" made only two pauses, which were too isolated for safety.

Market analysts are divided into two groups—fundamentalists and technical analysts. The former are concerned with earnings, management, gross national product (GNP), inflation, etcetera, while the latter analyze the market itself—that is, they don't try to outguess the big money but merely base their decisions on charts, tape reading, money-market studies, and so on. Actually there is no reason why the two approaches cannot complement each other—except in a major bear market. A major bear market is, by definition, the withdrawal of almost all fundamental support from the stock market—few want stock at any price during the height of the selling.

Unfortunately, such misinterpretations as the "speculation" theory of 1929 prevailed. Speculation did not cause the spectacular rises. There was firm, sound financial support until the big volume blowoffs in 1929 and 1965–67. We simply were riding too high and had too far to fall.

One naive criticism that will no doubt be heard, at least occasionally, is that the Vietnam War was engineered by Wall Street to stimulate the economy. This is obvious nonsense. The war bloody well panicked Wall Street. If the situation turns out to be as bad as the trend indicates, criticism of Wall Street will again rise to a crescendo. It would be an entirely useless gesture to suspend trading after the market had already bottomed out. As a matter of fact, the stock market merely shows in the most graphic way possible the extent to which investment money has been withdrawn from the economy. The market can and should be used by government to determine when the economy is developing at an overheated pace. And conversely, professional analysis of the bond market can tell us when government fiscal policy is unwise in its use of credit (deficit spending). It is a major misfortune that these lessons were not learned before. But our misunderstanding of the financial world was exaggerated by historians. We have seen how the idea of "speculation" was developed as a cause of the crash in 1929. No less a person than John Kenneth Galbraith erroneously blames "speculation," which he fails to define adequately, as a cause of The Great Crash. (The closest thing to an adequate explanation of the '29 crash that I have read is in Robert T. Patterson's *The Great Boom and Panic*, Chicago: Henry Regnery, 1965.) The analyst who would explain the cause of a money panic *must* be technically oriented, for the causes are entirely technical. Even those detractors of a technical approach to the stock market in normal times have no valid argument for a fundamental approach to the market in a panic. Fundamental rules are in fact completely reversed in panics. If volume increases as the market rises when support is withdrawn, this may be indicative of a major selloff rather than a bullish future for the market. The market may crash when business is excellent. Note, for instance, the following headlines from the front page of the *Wall Street Journal* of September 3, 1929, the day the bull market ended:

TRANSCONT OIL INCOME GAINING
 WITH CONTINUED GOOD OUTPUT, QUARTER &
  9 MONTHS SHOW
 SHARP INCREASE
  BETTER CAPITAL SETUP

AMERICAN CAN BEST YEAR SEEN
 OPERATIONS WELL AHEAD OF LAST YEAR—
 GAIN OF 25% IN NET INDICATED
  STOCKHOLDERS TO PROFIT

MAIL ORDER RECORD
 MONTGOMERY WARD AUGUST SALES JUMP 46.7%
 BIGGEST GAIN IN COMPANY'S HISTORY

 By the same token, the sophisticated stock trader always ends up with a good deal of undeserved blame in a major bear market. If he was cognizant enough to foresee the decline, he is blamed for accelerating the decline by going short. At the same time the trader who got caught and was long receives blame for boosting prices with undue "speculation." To blame any and all who are in the stock market at the time of a panic is nonsense. As a matter of fact, the stock trader serves a function by taking the edge off the excesses of the market. If he wants to sell short, he must do so only while his stock is rising. Thus his short sale would, if anything, tend to keep the stock from rising even further before it took a serious fall. And he must eventually cover his short sale, which provides an automatic support for the stock and tends to keep the market in that stock from falling as far as it might otherwise. Hence we must not look immediately in front of our noses at the normal trading of the market place, but must look at the root and cause of the panic—the destruction of confidence in the credit of the government of the United States.

Liberal reformers find themselves at odds with Wall Street mainly because they misunderstand the market. Although in need of reasonable control, especially against fraud, the money markets are really the best barometer we have to tell us when we get too big for our own britches. The fact that they have not been used as such appears to be the fault of government, not of the markets.

The pros and cons of the war show us that our black-and-white monolith is not confined to reactionaries. Wall Street finds itself as unalterably opposed to the Vietnam War as is Berkeley; and the American Legion finds itself, by supporting the war, opposing big business. And as we shall see, the Left, by supporting big government, confuses its search for "identity" even more. The Right, by supporting the war, gives tacit approval to big government. Moderation is lost on all. The black-and-white dogmatism of the American people can be seen most clearly in all its uncompromising folly at such a time of crisis as today. By assuming such fixed allegiances rooted in the two poles of the past, we frequently find ourselves with wrong or imagined enemies. Pragmatism, reason, and a willingness to give up traditional alliances and hatreds offer the only ways to appraise situations as they arise. No individual in this nation has all his real interests completely aligned with either extreme at all times. Those uncompromising and traditional antagonisms are the very sources of violent totalitarianism.

If this panic is properly understood, it should be a political boon to fiscally conservative but pragmatic (concerned with poverty) peace candidates. (*Note:* As this book goes to press, the moderate Republicans led by Governor Nelson Rockefeller have already lost the nomination to Nixon, and it seems that it will be 1972 before such a candidate can assume the presidency. Since this book is current, it seems important to advise the reader about the dates of any revisions. This paragraph is being revised in early

September, 1968, a week after the Democratic Convention. There are no other revisions not mentioned in the Prologue.) In his appearance on a CBS-TV news special in the summer of 1967, Nixon stated that foreign policy was the number one issue—which was true—since it would take a genius to ruin the economy of the nation, which may also have been true; but it showed that Nixon was as unaware of the inner workings of government finance as the President. (When the economic situation in this nation becomes apparent, no doubt Mr. Nixon will lose no time in trying to twist the statement to his advantage: "I said just a short time ago that it would take a genius to ruin the nation's economy, and the Democratic President . . ." or something to that effect.)²³ Nixon, of course, is a dangerous man in that he combines a Dulles-like foreign policy with an oily, homespun double-talk which appeals to those who cannot see through him. As an apostle of the extreme Right, he may be more dangerous than an outspoken candidate, such as Goldwater or Reagan. For whereas the latter two gentlemen persist in constantly putting their feet in their mouths, Nixon appears to slick-talk the public by changing his philosophy from one election to the next, depending upon what the mood of the public seems to be. Actually, Mr. Nixon may be more sincere, in a way, than is generally suspected. It appears not unlikely that this man may actually come to believe in his own rather wildly vacillating positions as he convinces the voters or delegates. If this is indeed true, it would indicate a frightening type of personality to have control of the nuclear trigger. This suspicion is reinforced by his notorious tantrum upon losing an election in 1962. Such symptoms are common to men obsessed with power and ambition who are poor losers. As for Hubert Humphrey, we are again given an unfortunate "choice" in 1968 as in 1964. In spite of Humphrey's tendency to spend, which would be unfortunate at a time like this, and in spite of his refusal to disassociate himself from President Johnson's Vietnam policy, it seems from this vantage point that Humphrey would be more likely to get out of Vietnam than Nixon and Nixon more

---

²³ There is substantial reason to believe that Nixon may be much wiser in the wiles of finance in the summer of 1968 than he was when he made the statement above.

likely to drop the bomb than Humphrey, although this is obviously unqualified opinion. While war and peace are the overriding issue and will always remain so as long as nuclear war is a threat, neither candidate seems likely to unite the country. Too many people, Americans and foreigners alike, view the current rash of violence in terms of black versus white. But the division and causes are not so simple as that. It seems to be a case of the entire country plunging toward totalitarianism—black *and* white and right *and* left—caused by a final victory of romantic over Enlightened philosophy. Such a profound problem at a time like this will present a formidable job for either man. History may view the current massive crisis as having begun with the assassination of John Kennedy. Perhaps Senator Edward Kennedy, who should be a serious presidential candidate in 1972, could come closest to pacifying the country if only because of his name. Senator McCarthy, who has become a national hero by playing a major part in bringing down the Johnson administration, should still be around in '72 as well. Senator George McGovern has shown the best understanding of all the candidates of either party of the major issues in 1968, including the fiscal and monetary crisis. And there are excellent men upon the Republican horizon—Senators Brooke, Hatfield, and Percy, Mayor Lindsay, and Governor Winthrop Rockefeller, to name a few.

Peace candidates might become more popular in the near future, and the money panic could end the war. But fiscally conservative congressmen who voted war credits without demur must share the blame with the administration for the mess we are in. For while lamenting the tremendous amount of irresponsible spending by the government, they continued to vote virtually unrestrained credits for Vietnam. The moderate Republicans in general and those Democrats who have been bold enough to speak out against a disastrous war must all be regarded as having emerged from our present predicament unsullied. In general, it is the warmongers, euphemistically called hawks, who, conservative and liberal spender alike, have violated the rules of government finance and created the presented situation.

The moderate doctrine does not preclude a Scandinavian type

of socialism. This could be the logical outcome of the pragmatic changes that might be deemed necessary for a particular country in a particular situation. However, the changes should be examined according to their individual merits and not in a preoccupation with who owns what rather than what will be the results of our changes. Denmark's economy could conceivably be based upon laissez faire, with what we call socialism having sprung from a practical pragmatism. We thus emerge with two basic rules for change: (1) Change must not be for the sake of change itself; but if after due consideration, a definite need for change exists, then act. (2) When making changes, hold all other things constant. Change only that particular thing for which a need for change has been demonstrated. Otherwise more harm than good may result.

The laissez faire of the Manchester school of economics represents economic anarchy if carried to extremes. This admission, however, should not tempt one to throw out the entire system and revert to a completely controlled economy which only invites totalitarian influences in other areas of society. Rather it demands moderate change and compromise.

The last quote from Palmer and Colton regarding the social changes arising from World War I brings us to an issue which is very much with us today—that which is euphemistically called the credibility gap. This is another way of saying that the administration lies to or withholds vital information from the voters. Such an unfortunate policy is an outgrowth of the propaganda efforts of all belligerents in the world wars. Whether and to what extent this high-pitched, officially sanctioned propaganda was necessary to prepare this country for all-out war is highly debatable. It might be argued, for instance, that no slanting of information was needed to arouse the American people to the German threat, at least in World War II, and that if one's national existence is at stake, no painting of the enemy as a demon is needed. In any case, the custom of propagandizing to the American people was not completely dropped in 1945. In a democracy sovereignty lies with the people. If it is to work, they *must* be informed in order to exercise the franchise. (Some leeway must be allowed in the area of diplomacy. The world of diplomacy functions in ways strange to most citizens of the twentieth century. The intricacies of diplomatic relations evolved through the centuries and it could prove unwise for all negotiations to be followed in detail by the public at the moment of occurrence, since the diplomat can often achieve better results when allowed to perform his work without undue scrutiny by the press.) Just as in the absolute monarchies, where the prime minister was required to report all important matters to the king in a truthful, precise manner, so must an administration report to a sovereign people in an unbiased manner the results of any and all information and decisions, including the reasons for such decisions. The relationship of the President to the people of the United States is exactly that of prime minister to king in an absolute monarchy. If the king is to run his country effectively, the prime minister must be honest in his reports to the crown; if he is not, he will be asked to resign. So it must be in a democracy. This is the very essence without which democratic government cannot function. A record of persistently lying to the press and the people, or withholding information that cannot reasonably be classified as militarily or diplomatically inadvisable to disclose, is and must be grounds for impeachment, or the republic cannot function.

Since World War II our government has persisted in the habit of withholding information that does not fall into these categories. During the Eisenhower years it was the policy of the administration to defend the testing of nuclear and thermonuclear devices and to assure the citizenry that the explosions were not creating harmful levels of radiation in the atmosphere, by suppressing information to the contrary. This was an insult to the maturity and intelligence of the sovereign people of this country. If the administration's policy was wise, then surely the people would have concurred. It is hardly likely that, in the immediate post-Stalin era, we would have become so concerned about fallout that we would have opted for cessation of tests to an extent which would have endangered our relative position.

If we had, it would have been our responsibility. Such perversion of facts is a complete reversal of the sovereign-servant relationship of the Jeffersonian concept of democratic government.

During his administration President Johnson and his cabinet have constantly deluded the people about that dark war in Vietnam. We are offered a plethora of double talk about the freedom of the South Vietnamese and the right of a free people to select their own government. It is virtually impossible to find an American in any walk of life who believes this blather. Those who support the war do so generally out of a blind anti-communism or a rather uninformed faith in the government. If we are to adopt Woodrow Wilson's idea of making the world safe for democracy—and it will be argued below that we should —then we must not delude ourselves about where democracy does and does not exist. This is the major distinction that many thinking Americans made when they advocated United States backing of Israel in the June, 1967, Middle Eastern war, even though they did not support the effort in Vietnam. There is only one reason to be in Vietnam, and President Johnson is obviously aware of this. If he is not, then we must despair of our leadership. That reason is the possibility that the so-called domino theory might be valid. Is Vietnam vital to the security of the British Commonwealth democracies, such as Australia and India, and to the United States itself? By considering such a vital question solely, the Vietnam War might still be deemed a necessary one. (It will be argued below that it is not.) The government of this country does the world a disservice by insulting the intelligence of the American people. If we are to develop into a sophisticated sovereign people capable of making decisions as leaders of the democratic world, then we must insist that our "prime minister" stop his double talk and show proper respect to his sovereign and the very concept of democracy by leveling with us.

There are those who think that we are morally right in Vietnam. (Moralism has been one of the shortcomings of our foreign policy throughout our history, and can be an especially disastrous characteristic when thermonuclear bombs are present.) It will not be argued here that we are morally wrong in Vietnam, for my view is that morals in this particular case are essentially irrelevant.[24]

Morals can and should dictate foreign policy any time national survival is not at stake. On the other hand, when national survival is involved, one must throw the rules of ordinary diplomacy and warfare out the window. The British bombardment of Copenhagen during the Napoleonic Wars is a case in point. Britain was the lone holdout against Napoleon, who had conquered the entire continent, just as Hitler did less than a century and a half later. Great Britain was fighting for her life. The Danes were sympathetic to the British, and the British committed a serious tactical error by bombarding Copenhagen. The decision was made by the admirals and not by the civilian government at home. Although Britain acquired some ships from the action, the incensed Danes allied themselves with the French. The action would ordinarily have been morally indefensible, but it was a matter of national survival. Since the action was also a tactical failure in the long run, it was a serious error. It is in such a light that we will examine Vietnam. Is it a sensible policy with regard to ensuring the existence of the Western-oriented democracies against anti-democratic expansionism? (Note that we do not call the enemy "communism," for there are other enemies. Readers might, in fact, find it interesting to substitute the term *totalitarianism* for both *fascism* and *communism* throughout the rest of this essay or in their vocabulary for a few days. How such a substitution will help truly focus the great political issue of the twentieth century will become clearer when we get to the definition of totalitarianism below.)

The press, of course, holds a responsible position in a working democracy. The role is so important that it is virtually the key to the success or failure of any democratic country. At this

---

[24] For those interested in the moral issues, there are many excellent, unbiased works. Notable is *Viet Nam*, edited by Marvin E. Gettleman and available in a Fawcett paperback (1965). One who studies the moral issues thoroughly must conclude that if the administration is to defend the war effort successfully, it must do so on other issues.

juncture our press seems to be becoming more responsible. There
are still too many irresponsible newspapers, but there are some
excellent ones—the New York *Times,* the *Wall Street Journal,* the
St. Louis *Constitution,* the Louisville *Courier-Journal,* and the
St. Louis *Post-Dispatch,* to name a few. A trend toward greater
sophistication of Americans in everything from dress to worldly
knowledge seems to have set in in the sixties, and this appears
to be due to television. But even on the national scale, the
press has occasionally not lived up to its responsibilities. I have
expressed a more favorable impression of the Cuban Revolution
than most Americans. The press, led by *Time* magazine, was
extremely unfair to the Cuban Revolution after 1959. Space does
not permit taking up that argument here in detail. Americans
who were able to remember from one month to the next,
however, saw a virulent press perverting the facts completely and
leading the American people like sheep in their attitudes toward
Cuba. In fact, Castro had first turned to the United States for
help. When he nationalized foreign-owned property, he compen-
sated the owners with bonds which could not be considered
worthless (and probably would not have been had the United
States cooperated somewhat) until the Cuban government
actually defaulted. Thus it was all quite legal under generally
accepted international law. Much private investment, at least at
that time, was still in private hands. The Cuban government
was so desperate to regain the respect of the United States
that it retained an American advertising agency to beef up its
image. It made every effort to cooperate with this government
while still maintaining its sovereignty.[25] It was all to no avail.
The American press ranted and raved for an overthrow of the
Cuban government. Lies and innuendoes abounded to an extent
not seen since William Randolph Hearst with his virulent journalism succeeded in getting this country into the Spanish-American
War—again involving Cuba—after Cuba had nearly won her revolution against Spain without outside aid.

---

[25] C. Wright Mills, *Listen Yankee* (New York: McGraw-Hill, 1960),
is still valuable for the historical perspective of the revolution.

With regard to Vietnam, the press has presented us with a different pattern. *Time* is one of the more militant popular organs in regard to that war. But basically the press has been rather fair. The fault here is more subtle. Even such unbiased and somewhat anti-war reporters as *Newsweek* and CBS have not analyzed in detail the moral issues involved in Vietnam. So the problem here is more one of a gap left unfilled with regard to a country about which most Americans were quite ignorant, rather than one of yellow journalism in the usual sense.

Time has misrepresented only certain issues in the past. These were ordinarily the pet projects of Henry Luce—Cuba, for instance, and, I strongly believe, Oswald's guilt. Ordinarily one only needed to be overly cautious of what he read in *Time* when that organ was discoursing on countries where few Americans traveled—Bulgaria or Southeast Asia as opposed to France and the United States.

As our press gave us only the right-wing side of the story in Cuba, they gave only the left-wing side of the story of the Franco-Algerian War, which was responsible for De Gaulle's rise to power. There was no hysterical ranting as in the case of Cuba. But there was a tremendous amount to be said for the French position in that conflict, and it remained basically unsaid.

Since Henry Luce's recent death, *Time* appears to have become more liberal. The organ that coined *vietnik* and other uncomplimentary names for the New Left has become surprisingly sympathetic toward that movement. And it seems that everyone forgets that *Time* supported John F. Kennedy against Richard Nixon in the 1960 election.

In regard to the assassination, the title *Rush to Judgement* is as appropriate a title as one could imagine. The haste that the press, and especially *Time*, displayed in assuming Oswald's guilt was so indecorous as to make it appear they were conspirators themselves. (This is doubtful. Kennedy was *Time's* golden boy. But, perhaps to avert possible civil war, they reported to us that a yet untried theory was true.) The popular press has persisted in jumping to conclusions in such instances as the Garrison investigation in New Orleans—the same shortcoming for which they fault the New Orleans district attorney. (One may note such suspicious coincidences as Garrison's assistant William Gurvich denouncing his boss immediately after a visit by Robert Kennedy.) As the assassination and its aftermath unfolded before the eyes of the American people, it was reminiscent of a scene in George Orwell's *Animal Farm*. In that satirical book the rules of society are painted on the barn after the revolution. Such laws as "No animal shall sleep in a bed" and "No animal shall kill another animal" are thus promulgated. As the pigs rise to power, they lose the idealism of the early days of the revolution and begin to sleep in Farmer Jones's bed and kill some of the more unruly of the other animals. The sign on the barn is stealthily changed to "No animal shall sleep in a bed *without sheets*" and "No animal shall kill another animal *without cause.*" Although the paint is still fresh, the other animals shake their heads and decide it must have been that way all along. Such was the spectacle of the American people watching the assassination aftermath unfold and deciding Oswald's guilt (as they had Castro's guilt). Perhaps one enlightening revelation would be to show films of the entire assassination story over nationwide television. (*Author's note*: See the excellent feature article on the Garrison investigation in the January, 1968, issue of *Ramparts*. As this book goes to press in the aftermath of the assassinations of Dr. Martin Luther King and Sen. Robert Kennedy and a general wave of violence throughout the land, one can't help but wonder how different the situation might be today if the full story of President Kennedy's murder had been disclosed.)

As we have seen, anti-Semitism in Germany was rooted in romanticism. The Young Germany movement, a literary movement of about 1820, was discredited by traditional German society because of the high number of Jews in its ranks. (Compare German anti-Semitism and anti-intellectualism with the reactionary slogan to "register Communists, not firearms" and the World War II registration of Jews by the National Socialists, as well as the frequent attempts to discredit the civil-rights movement by falsely claiming that it is communist-dominated.)

A monument to the great Jewish lyric poet Heinrich Heine ". . . which his admirers wished to set up for him in his native Düsseldorf wandered, unwanted, from Düsseldorf to Mainz to Hamburg to Berlin, until it finally found a resting place on the Grand Concourse in the Bronx, in New York City."[26]

Ludwig Börne of the Young Germany movement wrote:

It is like a miracle! A thousand times have I experienced it and yet it is eternally new to me. Some reproach me because I am a Jew; others excuse me for it; a third praises me for it. But all of them think of it. They are as though they were fixed by the spell of this magic Jewish circle and no one can get out. I also know quite well where this evil charm comes from. The poor Germans! Living in the lowest floor, oppressed by the seven floors of the upper classes, their anxiety is made lighter by speaking of people who are still lower than they are and who live in the cellar. Not being a Jew provides them with consolation at not being a state councillor. No, the fact that I was born a Jew has not embittered me against the Germans and has never deluded me. I would indeed not be worthy to enjoy the light of the sun if I paid with scornful grumbling for the great act of grace that God has shown me of letting me be both a German and a Jew. Only because of the derision that I have always scorned and because of the suffering that I have long since ceased to feel . . . yes, because I was a bondsman, I therefore love liberty more than you. Yes, because I have known slavery, I understand freedom more than you. Yes, because I was born without a fatherland my desire for a fatherland is more passionate than yours, and because my birthplace was not bigger than the *Judengasse* [Jew Alley] and everything behind the locked gates was a foreign country to me, therefore, for me now the fatherland is more than the city, more than a territory, more than a province. For me only the very great fatherland, as far as its language extends, is enough. . . . And because I am no longer the bondsman of citizens I also do not wish to remain any longer the slave of princes. I want to be completely free again. I have built my house

---

[26] *Pinson*, op. cit., p. 70.

of freedom from bottom up; do as I have done and do not feel
content with covering the roof of a rotten political edifice with
new tiles."[27]

The relationship between the Jew in Germany and the Negro
in America is obvious in Börne's writings. Even among participants in the revolution of 1848, anti-Semitism was to be found.
Witness this statement from Pinson:

> The more radical member [of the Liberal Parliament of the
> South German states] also met together to frame their . . . de-
> mands. Sometimes such programs combined radical political
> and social slogans with antisemitic charges against Jews. As fre-
> quently happened in many of the cruder expressions of social
> protest in Europe, the Jews were looked upon as the chief agents
> of commercial and capitalistic exploitation. . . .
> . . . Very frequently these economic and political aspirations
> were combined with antisemitic agitation against the Jews.
> Peasant revolts broke out throughout rural Germany in the early
> months of 1848. The most serious occurred in the Odenwald and
> Black Forest regions. This area, decidedly feudal in character
> and peopled by a heavily burdened peasantry, began its agrarian
> revolts with anti-Jewish outbreaks . . . One peasant leaflet pro-
> claimed the goal of the revolution to be (1) the destruction of
> the nobility, (2) the banishment of all Jews from Germany,
> (3) the elimination of all kings, dukes, and princes and the con-
> version of Germany into a free state like America, and (4) the
> execution of all officials.[28]

This discussion of anti-Semitism in 1848 necessitates some
mention of the relationship of the American Negro to the 1776
revolution. He was, of course, completely left out. This was a
result of four conditions. (1) European society as a whole,
however amazing it may seem today, had not abolished the
institution of slavery—especially in its colonies. Since the American colonies were included in this slave-trading area of the
British Empire, they inherited the problem. (2) Many northern

[27] *Gesammelte Schriften* (Milwaukee, 1858), Vol. V, pp. 31-32, as
quoted in Pinson.
[28] Pinson, *op. cit.*, pp. 81, 83.

delegates to the Constitutional Convention wished to abolish slavery. It was a burning issue. But foremost in their minds (as in the Civil War eighty-five years later) was the Union. The northern Liberals hoped to solve the problem of slavery after the country was established. In fact, there was something to be said for the stand that slavery could not be abolished in the South by northerners until the two areas became one country. (3) As mentioned above, American slavery, according to contemporary historians, is considered to have been the most degrading in the history of the world.[29] This may have been a result of the fact that (4) the typical white inhabitant of the Deep South was even less enlightened than he is today. And in the nineteenth and twentieth centuries, romanticism had a deep effect on the American South as it did on Germany.[30]

Those who studied United States history before 1959, when Mr. Elkins's book was published, were taught two other misconceptions which were foisted upon the American public by slavery apologists near the turn of the century: (1) that slavery was *not* the main cause of the Civil War, and (2) that Reconstruction was a completely unenlightened, vindictive policy on the part of the North. The first point is rather obvious in retrospect, for it is hard to imagine a nation that was able to compromise its vast differences in order to unite in the first place becoming so sharply and tragically divided over the amount of the tariffs. The second point, however, is for obvious reasons more sharply disputed among reputable historians. The new view is that our problems with the South remain today to a great extent because Reconstruction did not last long enough and was not pervasive enough. This brings us to a Liberal dilemma: what to do with a conquered land, such as Germany or the American South, when the division that splits victor and vanquished is as basic as in these two examples. It is understandably against the grain of the Liberal with his espousal of freedom of thought to teach children in German or southern schools to think

[29] See p. 47, footnote.
[30] See Rollin G. Osterweis, *Romanticism and Nationalism in the Old South* (New Haven: Yale Univ. Press, 1949).

like Americans or northerners, or to force democracy upon them
if their people in the majority would prefer absolute monarchy or
dictatorship. Yet we suffer today from the failure of our ancestors
to change the South. After the North lost hundreds of thousands
of men for the cause of the American Negro, it failed to consolidate its victory. What reconstruction existed certainly had serious
shortcomings, although this was greatly exaggerated by earlier
historians. By the same token we shall soon see how again the
failure of German Liberals to consolidate their power by suppressing reaction in the schools and elsewhere in the years of the
Weimar Republic (1919–1933) contributed substantially to the
rise of Adolf Hitler and National Socialism. (Young American
liberals, in a natural revulsion from the reactionary policies of
the House Committee on Un-American Activities and other
abusive arms of Congress, frequently object to taking oaths of
loyalty to the Constitution. This is a serious tactical error. The
oath should be taken proudly and the tables quickly turned on the
reactionaries.)

Nor was Abraham Lincoln as much a friend to the Negro as is
generally thought. (Stokely Carmichael has a point.) Certainly
there were those whites who considered the Negro their equal;
but an examination of Lincoln's speeches will show that he was
not one of them. The Negro did have true friends among
American Presidents, however. The slaveowner Thomas Jefferson
mended his ways, released his slaves, and appeared to be sincere
about it; in fact, among American patriarchs, Jefferson probably
stands up under scrutiny better than any other. Slave owners
may seem hard to forgive in the late twentieth century, and the
only argument in their behalf is that they were a product of their
times. This will fail to satisfy many Negroes; but it can be pointed
out that it is just as hard for the American white to understand
a people that took a full century to assert themselves after release from slavery. Both were products of historical accident.
Certainly the actions of Eisenhower, John Kennedy, and, in all
fairness, Johnson have shown them to be decisive and affirmative
on behalf of civil rights. This still will not be enough for many
Negro people to feel that the American Revolution is somehow

theirs. It is, of course, though it has been for only a few years—since they made it theirs in 1961. It is now completely at the disposal of those who wish to adopt it. The white moderates and liberals (to use a term in disrepute in this sense) cannot be bothered apologizing for the white race. A German Social Democrat who did everything possible throughout the Nazi period to resist must put himself to better use than spending his life apologizing for the vast majority of the German people. The American white who has no anti-Negro feeling is extremely rare. They do, of course, exist. These people have no white brothers; they may not even feel that we are all brothers under the skin, but perhaps that people as a whole are no damned good. In any event, their immediate hope is usually to make all Americans first-class citizens. At the moment that seems possible only by fighting both reaction and radicalism together. On the surface it seems to make little practical difference to the true white liberal whether he helps in the civil-rights movement or not. If the Negro wants to go it alone, that is his business. But the viciousness of much of the reactionary movement in this country could result in a counterrevolution as vicious as the Nazi movement. If that day comes, let us hope that Negroes and sympathetic whites can be good friends. And let us hope that our Commander in Chief and our military have taken their oaths to the Constitution seriously.

As we have seen, just as anti-Negro feeling has virtually always been a part of American life, so anti-Semitism has long been a part of German life. By the late nineteenth century, the more radical anti-Semitic feeling was expressed by the composer Richard Wagner. Wagner was one of Hitler's favorite "philosophers." In actuality Wagner should have stuck to his music, for he did little to further even the most unsavory philosophy. He did, however, epitomize much that was sick about Germany.

> "Emancipation from the yoke of Judaism appears to us the foremost necessity," Wagner wrote. "Above all we must prove our strength in this war of liberation. Now we shall never gain this strength from abstract concepts, but only . . . from our feeling an instinctive repugnance of the Jewish character. Thus . . . it will

become plain to us what we hate . . . through this exposure we may hope to rout the demon from the field where he can exist only in the shelter of a twilight darkness—a darkness we good-natured humanitarians have cast upon him ourselves, to make his look less loathsome." As early as 1851 Wagner wrote Liszt: "I have cherished a long repressed resentment about this Jew business, and this grudge is as necessary to my nature as gall is to the blood." Jews—directly or through their influence tolerated by unsuspecting gentiles—were responsible for Germany's decay, for the degradation of art, above all for opposition to Wagner. Cosima [Wagner's wife] almost surpassed her husband in interpreting all contemporary history as a plot of Jews (and sometimes of Catholics) to destroy Germanic civilization, Wagner, and world salvation. Both agreed with the position taken by some Jewish nationalists, that a Jew was not a German or a European and could not think and create as a German. Jews remained forever aliens in their European homelands; by unbreakable mystical ties they belonged to their race and their distant ancestral soil.[31]

Jews were defined by one German anti-Semitic writer as anyone with a drop of Jewish blood—an extravagant definition with a familiar American-segregationist ring. Frau Wagner's rabid extremism makes us think of many Republican women who surpass their husbands in seeing communists in every alley. With this group of women on one hand and the Bobby Kennedy fad on the other, it sometimes seems we made a mistake in giving women the right to vote.[32]

World War I was, to a great extent, a result of the career of Otto von Bismarck, one of the great Germans of all times. The Iron Chancellor, the blood-and-iron philosopher, unified Germany in the period 1866–71 by rising to power in Prussia as a result of a conflict between Parliament and King. He accomplished the unification by means of successful wars against Denmark, Austria, and France, in that order. When France capi-

---

[31] Kohn, *op. cit.*, pp. 203-4.

[32] The reference to Robert Kennedy was meant only facetiously, to imply that the Senator was generally more popular with women than men.

tulated in 1870, Bismarck's forces caused the German Empire to be proclaimed in the Hall of Mirrors in Versailles, the equivalent of forcing the United States to kowtow to a conquering nation at the foot of the Washington monument. The excitement generated by Bismarck's fantastic military success made it an easy matter for all Germany to be united under Prussia in a federation of monarchies.

Bismarck ruled as Chancellor until 1890. A Prussian Junker who had been a little-known candidate to the Frankfurt assembly, he became the virtual dictator of all Germany. In 1888, William I, the German Emperor since Bismarck had made him such, died. His successor, Frederick III, was already critically ill. He ascended and died in three months' time. William II then ascended the throne. He was a different kind of man from William I and could not get along with his Chancellor. Bismarck was asked to step down two years after the death of William I.

We are here concerned with Bismarck's foreign policy and the void created in European diplomacy by his resignation. Bismarck had constructed a complicated network of foreign alliances which he handled well. His policy was essentially unwarlike in character. After conquering France and uniting Germany, he had accomplished his principal goal and set out on a long period of peaceful relationships. He organized the Triple Alliance with Italy and his former enemy, Austria. He maintained friendly ties with Germany's great natural enemy, Russia. He had no interest in uniting German-speaking peoples any further. He even achieved a détente with everybody's sometime enemy, Britain. He encouraged the expansion of other European powers in Asia and Africa to lessen tensions in Central Europe, and he succeeded in keeping France isolated. In sum, the world witnessed nearly twenty years of remarkable diplomatic acrobatics.

There were of course other factors involved in the causes of World War I, not the least of which was the simple fact that a century without a major war just seemed too much for Europe to bear. When Bismarck stepped down he left a diplomatic maze that his successors were not able to negotiate. World War I could be called the War of the Bismarckian Succession.

A vital part of German character in its outlook toward foreign countries had always been a paranoia which resembles that in the United States' official attitude toward communism in the John Foster Dulles era, and still governs much of American policy today. Germany was surrounded by enemies, or so she felt. France was on one side and Russia on the other. Britain's policy of keeping control of the seas was designed in part to keep Germany virtually landlocked. This paranoia became part of official German policy after Bismarck. Germany entered into a naval race against the British to build up her navy and thus offended the British, whose centuries-old policy of maintaining control of the seas as assurance against invasion was threatened. Crises developed involving German claims in Africa and the Balkans which would no doubt have been completely avoided under Bismarck.

The long-standing debate regarding blame for World War I remains unresolved. The immediate fault is Austria's, with a strong assist from Germany, but the underlying issues are a different matter. It is not our purpose to theorize on that debate nor to trace the complicated diplomatic tangles which led up to it. We shall examine, instead, some of the forces at work within Germany during that great war.

All Germany, except for a handful of pacifists, entered the war enthusiastically. The Socialists, who were ordinarily pacifistic, voted as a solid bloc for the war credits. (Thus the German Social Democrats demonstrated that in time of crisis they were capable of putting dogma aside; this in turn helped alienate the Bolsheviks from German Socialists in later years.) All parties ceased their bickering and united behind the government in support of the war. The liberal economist and social reformer Max Weber stated the feelings of most Germans. "This war," he wrote, "with all its ghastliness is nevertheless grand and wonderful. It is worth experiencing."[33]

The war plan, called the Schlieffen plan, called for a lightning sweep through Belgium and France and the capture of Paris within a few weeks. The Germans reasonably hoped that Britain

---

[33] *Gesammelte politische Schriften* (Munich, 1921), p. 458.

would remain neutral. Then, with the Western front freed, the German armies would be free to turn their attention to the Eastern front, for it would take Russia some time to mobilize. Soldiers marching to the Western front at the outbreak of the war were greeted by milling, cheering, flag-waving civilians who, as someone put it, confused the beginning of a disastrous world war with a national holiday.

Most Germans believed that the war, which started in August, 1914, would be over by Christmas. Defeats, setbacks, and stale-mates were closely guarded secrets. The German public were led to believe right up until November, 1918, that the war was going in their favor. The fact that the prolongation of the war did not lead the people to question their government's credibility is sur-prising to many. But with such bland assurances from press and government alike, the German people believed all was going smoothly almost until they saw the German armies retreating in all-out panic from the direction in which they had marched some four years earlier. Thus the myth of the "stab in the back" was easy to foist upon a people who had long been denied the facts, and was to become a major rallying cry of the Nazi party.

The Supreme Command instituted a rigorous censorship and clamped down on all news items that would have raised doubts as to ultimate German victory. The military leaders, however, showed little understanding for propaganda and psychological warfare. Practically all the daily reports spoke only of victories. Defeats were either suppressed entirely or so reported that only a few experts could grasp the true situation. The most glaring instance of this was the complete suppression in Germany of the true effect of the battle of the Marne in 1914. All that the Su-preme Command allowed the German public to know about this crucial battle was the following: "On the western front, opera-tions regarding which it is not yet possible to publish details have led to a new battle, which is going favorably. All the un-favorable reports being spread by the enemy through various means are false."

The famous economist Lujo Brentano tells how doubly grieved he was when he came to Florence, Italy, at the end of September, 1914. Here he learned for the first time about the true character of this decisive battle, and when he returned to Munich four weeks later and assumed that by that time all his colleagues knew all about it he was treated as one who had fallen an easy prey to enemy propaganda. Even the highest circles in civilian life were fed with a continuous string of glowing reports of victory, of promises of enormous gains for Germany as a result of the war, and were subjected to a complete blackout on all indications of any serious concern. Expression of sympathy for the hungry and suffering German people was banned by the military censorship. All descriptions of want of food or clothing or other physical suffering were forbidden. The official motto was, "No one can beat us!"

Such a manipulation of public opinion bred a dangerous state of confidence that was not justified by the facts . . . And when collapse finally did come it found the German people completely unprepared for it and dazed by the news of total defeat after they had been led all the time to believe that total victory was well in hand. [Ernst] von Heydebrand, the leader of the Conservative party, ran up and down and shouted, "We have been deceived and cheated," when the news of the request for an armistice came to him.[84]

Historians are fond of discussing German war aims in World War I. Actually Germany had no concrete aims. War aims were debated in the Reichstag, in the press, in the universities, and on the streets. People, parties, and other groups changed their war goals as fast as the situation at the front changed. When they thought they were winning, Germans leaned more toward the expansionist philosophies of the Pan-German party; when they sensed military misfortune, they leaned toward the attitude that theirs was a defensive war and all they wanted was their integrity.

The general feeling most Germans had from the start was that they were fighting a defensive war. All sides were essentially ignorant of the causes of the war, which came to light only after historians were able to piece together information from diplomatic files in the relative calm of the postwar years. With the all-pervasive propaganda at an extreme pitch for the first time in

---

[84] Pinson, *op. cit.,* p. 321.

world history—a propaganda that was the forerunner of such familiar things as totalitarianism and credibility gaps—the German people sincerely believed the Allies were plotting to destroy Germany or at least German interests. Germany, we noted earlier, had always exhibited a unique paranoia about foreigners and foreign affairs. She was surrounded by enemies, or so she felt. Russia was out to unite the Slavic peoples and attack her from the east. France, on the southwest, was even more of a natural enemy. Britain was always trying to keep Germany suppressed because a powerful Germany—a Germany which realized her true destiny—would threaten Britain's long cherished command of the seas, and her colonial interests. Most foreign nations wanted to keep Germany as landlocked as possible in order to confine her. Thus she dangerously demonstrated poor taste in foreign affairs and diplomacy in the post-Bismarckian years—a brinkmanship which nearly caused World War I to start early at least twice in the period after 1890 over issues regarding Africa. When the war finally did break out, there was no trouble in getting the Germans to believe that it was a war of aggression carried out by an international movement to conquer and subvert Germany.

The similarity between that German outlook toward the world and the current American outlook toward the world in general, and communism in particular, is all too striking. John Foster Dulles stands out in this regard, but other administrators display a notable German bluster, with slight trace of English maturity regarding power. If there is any element of safety to be found in a nuclear-armed world, it can be achieved only when the major powers find the maturity and responsibility that must go hand in hand with world leadership. In America it will be achieved only when the electorate in general finds that maturity. A preoccupation with communism as a monolithic bloc must give way to a calm, pragmatic view of that bloc as communism splits off into national and multinational units, matures in places, and becomes more like the Western democracies.

Annexationist aims in Germany were espoused by most politically powerful groups except the Socialists. This included the

Supreme Command, which took over the reins of government from the emperor as the war persisted. This annexationist view varied in detail. One Progressive leader (Friedrich Naumann) proposed in 1914 that Belgium be divided and given to France, Luxembourg, Holland, and Germany. The more extreme view was expressed by Ernst Bassermann, the leader of the National Liberals: "Where a drop of German blood has flowed there we remain." Many people throughout Germany took up this sentiment.

This brings us to another pause to compare American policy. German war aims may have been somewhat more sensible at first, but as soon as German blood was spilled, people's attitudes greatly changed. Even informed Germans could no longer see the war with an unbiased eye. (We see this same pattern in America regarding the Vietnam War.) Just as the great Woodrow Wilson in this country advocated "peace without victory," or a reasonable peace settlement *before* the United States entered the war, his demeanor changed to a great extent *after* this nation became embroiled. So, too, did the Germans make a moral issue out of a war in which no basic moral issue was involved. To make any reasonable observations and conclusions about war aims and diplomatic desirabilities for the next generation or more to come, one must divorce from his mind the fact that his countrymen have lost their lives fighting for those goals. This approach was usually taken in the period 1648–1914 (with the exception of the Napoleonic Wars). Wars were ended as easily as they were started and participants changed allegiances as easily as not. There was certainly a cynicism in this system, but moralism and ideology did not often become involved in war aims, and the world was much safer for it. Such ideological wars have developed in the twentieth century partly as a result of large-scale propaganda techniques. To maintain some perspective, a warring nation must not permit itself to become too emotional about the loss of its soldiers. In the Vietnam War, for instance, the American people need to be able to view things unemotionally. This extends to the very desirability of carrying the war any further (apart from whether or not that war is a mistake). The advantages that are possibly to be gained versus the disadvantages must be examined outside the atmosphere of an American Legion Vietnam Day parade. We, like the Germans, tend to confuse war with a national holiday. We would certainly achieve a better image if, upon finding that we had made a serious mistake, we were willing to admit that mistake with humility, even though American soldiers had fallen, than if we stubbornly insisted on carrying it to its logical conclusion. As long as a majority of the American people believe what the administration says about fighting for freedom rather than realize the sobering fact that we are fighting for a particular theory—the domino theory—of national survival, the people cannot decide the war upon its merits. Propaganda may have its uses in an unlimited war, such as World War II, although even then its desirability is questionable because of the danger of not being able to rid the government of the habit after the war is won, and the danger of a gross misunderstanding like the German myth of the stab in the back if the war is lost.

Among the several distinctions between unlimited and limited war is the fact that in the case of unlimited war it is desirable to occupy a country for a generation after its surrender. The American Civil War, a total war against a society alien to the victor's, should have been followed by occupation of the conquered area to root out the very causes. The problems so often attributed to Reconstruction are due mainly to the fact that Reconstruction was not really constructive and was not complete. The Negro needed to be educated—not just freed—worked into the electorate, and given an opportunity to gain political office as he became literate. The southern schools needed to be controlled enough to ensure that an effort was made to educate the next generation to accept the Negro. Integration should have been enforced completely (while maintaining non-racial distinctions, as in literacy) at gunpoint during the Andrew Johnson administration rather than during the Eisenhower administration. The Little Rock incident of September, 1957, and the necessity for the National Guard to protect marchers in Selma, Alabama, in February, 1965, proved the truth of the old slogan, "The South will rise again." In Germany the Weimar Republic made one of its major mistakes in not stamping out reaction with benevolent but firm power. Just as the old enemy, the Confederate South, is rearing its head in an ugly form today, so Germany rose again after World War I in a much uglier form as a result of an Allied war policy that was so engrossed with self-righteous moralism as to issue an unbelievably stern *diktat* at the end of the war, thus providing the principal issue for the Nazi rise to power. (The Allies did not even concern themselves with whether or not the Liberal Weimar Republic remained in control to stem the reactionary flood.) An unlimited war is a war against the people, civilian as well as military. One United States general recently stated that we would probably have to stay in Vietnam for twenty years or more. Apparently we intend to prove Rudyard Kipling wrong when he said that the twain shall never meet. If we are not prepared to tackle this valiant exercise in egocentricity, then the war must be kept on a limited scale; otherwise it will surely backfire, both from world opinion and within Vietnam itself. Today's Europeans (and Americans) are understandably oriented toward total war with all its propaganda. Most of us grew up during a period when total war was predominant and propaganda prevailed, reaching its logical, extreme conclusion in totalitarianism. But perhaps it is time to examine the days before this century, as Edmund Burke would no doubt advocate, in a search for a nuclear-age philosophy of war and peace. Our present outlook certainly needs some fresh ideas, old or new.

Another difference between total war and limited war and periods of peace can be found in attitudes toward the draft. Too many of our citizens fail to understand the distinction between 1941–45 and the post-1945 period regarding conscription. In the World War II period the draft was not initiated until a short time before we entered the war, when it was already apparent that the existence of our civilization was being menaced by a totalitarian regime which would impose an Eastern or medieval society upon us. Public opinion was almost unanimously with the war effort in the face of this threat. The constant propaganda picturing Hitler, Mussolini, Tojo, and Hirohito as ogres was essentially superfluous; America would undoubtedly have backed the war effort without such propaganda tactics. It is essential for those of us who are old enough to be veterans of the world wars to examine the differences between that situation and the post-1945 draft. The atmosphere surrounding the idea of military conscription has not been one of meeting a specific emergency but rather one of *universal military training*. There is no feeling of fighting for national survival, no air of urgency, except the always pervading horror of nuclear holocaust. Even during the Vietnam War it seems objectionable to many that they are required to fight a war in a country that the average soldier had never even heard of until the United States became seriously involved in that faraway quarrel. Many are afraid that we are unnecessarily becoming entangled in another fight for national survival. The apparent lack of enthusiasm may or may not be due to an underlying rejection of the domino theory. In any case, the concept of a permanent draft as opposed to a draft presumably "for the duration of the war and six months afterwards" must be considered in a completely different light. No draft is ever unpopular when it is raised by a popular government in the face of a struggle for existence. Drafts in countries which are major powers seem always to be unpopular when they become permanent policy. Small countries with a special pride in their identity, such as Switzerland, seem to be able to generate enough popular support for a limited amount of universal military training to be able to preserve it to some advantage—perhaps out of an awareness of their relative lack of power in time of emergency. Israel is an example of a nation which is able to combine both this type of support and an enthusiasm for the draft, engendered by a permanent and real threat to her existence from the Arab states. France, on the other hand, grew so disenchanted with her draft and state of permanent war since the 1930's that by the 1950's the anti-draft forces broke out in near open rebellion during the Algerian War—a war that obviously didn't threaten the existence of mainland France, just as the Indochinese independence movement did not threaten the French way of life. These young Frenchmen felt the natural repulsion that most people who are rooted in the philosophy of the Enlightenment feel toward infringements upon their personal freedoms. Few would object to being called in real emergency; few can tolerate such a thing as a permanent governmental doctrine.

One may note that in many cases those who most vociferously support the current draft are the very ones who, this book implies throughout, are in direct philosophical *counterrevolution to the American Revolution*—alienated from the ideas of Locke and Jefferson and Rousseau and in sympathy with ideas which stem not from our heritage but from Eastern totalitarianism and medieval culture. This is not to imply that a support of the draft alone makes one a counterrevolutionary; but a preponderance of ideas of the type espoused by the extreme Right and by the few of the extreme Left does put one in direct conflict with the American Revolution.

Some statements from "respectable" reactionaries will help to illustrate the point:

> "Let's deal with these buzzards," cried Democratic Rep. L. Mendel Rivers of South Carolina. "Nothing is too strong for them." Nevada Democrat Walter S. Barring called them "dirty, longhaired, Communist-led beatniks." "Take them about 200 miles in the ocean," urged Florida's Democratic Congressman James A. Haley. "Handcuff them with their hands behind their backs, chain the anchor around their neck, throw them overboard and tell them to swim to any country that they want whose flag they can respect . . . We'll let the courts worry about the Constitution," [said one unnamed Congressman.][35]

Now, this particular example of congressional invective happened after a flag-burning incident, which involved only two or three people at a large peace demonstration. Few will doubt that burning the United States flag is certainly in bad taste, and some may feel that it may actually harm the cause of peace in Vietnam. Many may even share my view that it should probably be a misdemeanor—disorderly conduct—with a fine of not more

---

[35] "Burned Up," *Newsweek*, July 3, 1967, p. 29. Copyright, Newsweek, Inc., July, 1967.

than ten to twenty-five dollars.[36] We have here, nevertheless, quite a number of statements which are, to put it mildly, unbecoming to congressmen. Nazis and romanticists in Germany had their Jews, and their American counterparts seem to have their Negroes, and their "dirty, long-haired, Communist-led beatniks" who should be eliminated—taken "200 miles out in the ocean," handcuffed "with their hands behind their backs," with an anchor chained about their necks, and thrown overboard. Such bad taste on the part of both demonstrators as well as congressmen only aggravates the problems. If American people would stop sending men to Congress who are likely to reciprocate a gesture of bad taste by a single youth or a handful of youths with ugly gestures of even worse taste, one could feel a bit more optimistic generally about the future.

Returning to the draft, the real, practical danger in forcing men to submit to a truly unpopular draft is that if a real national crisis similar to World War II did develop, years of unwise conscription might prove to have dealt a serious blow to the possibility of again achieving that natural spontanteous burst of patriotism to which Western society owes its existence. A true patriot will rise to the occasion when he feels he is needed; but it is not necessarily indicative of a lack of patriotism for a youth not to want to be drafted unless he is convinced that his country and society are being immediately threatened or the things he cherishes are endangered. A draftee hardly feels that he is saving his country if he spends his two years sitting in a finance office at Fort Knox computing military pay. It is easy in such circumstances to feel that the American people simply do not want to spend the money to hire a woman from the civilian labor force as a replacement. One can sometimes wonder if perhaps the typical citizen isn't more concerned about a new appliance for

---

[36] Anything much stricter would be reminiscent of the current fad of imposing unreasonable fines for littering—a crime for which we may eventually see some state impose the death penalty. Surely there is a point of diminishing returns in the imposition of penalties where a rebellious minority will begin to adopt a particular crime to which an unreasonable penalty is attached as a symbol of rebellion.

his home than about the freedom of those of draft age. This idea is reinforced by the millions of American men who are against the draft until after they serve their time and then seem to feel that everyone should go because they did.

Some have argued that it would be more equitable to draft, as a few countries already do, young people of both sexes regardless of physical limitations. A man with one leg, so the argument runs, can serve his military obligation at a desk outside the battle zone; women can do many of the more menial tasks, releasing able-bodied men for combat or more arduous physical labor; the feeble-minded would make good KP's. Certainly a system similar to this works in Israel. As we have seen, however, Israel is in a different situation, as shown by the ready, even enthusiastic, acceptance of such service. If Israeli foreign affairs ever relaxed enough to permit a concomitant relaxation of the draft, and if the government did not subsequently relax the draft laws accordingly, a new generation of Israelis would no doubt come along which would openly rebel against conscription. It seems, then, that there is probably a direct correlation between the desirability of a draft and the acceptance of it. When rumblings against the draft become loud, it is time for government policy makers to review the situation to see if the draft is still desirable. When enough people feel the draft is unneeded, perhaps it really is. The objection to the above system of true universal military service is obvious. Such a system would be a basic infringement upon the freedom of choice of the Western-oriented citizen unless true emergency required an unusual, temporary sacrifice of that freedom to ensure the future. One must occasionally maintain some principle even in the face of real danger. A system basically free of the imposition of a permanent draft seems worth this sacrifice. If the universal military service outlined above, which in our example had already been extended to include everyone, were carried further, the only direction left would be to extend the length of service. If this step were carried to a logical conclusion, the length of service would be extended as indefinitely as our present "permanent state of emergency." We would then have a system as pervasive as in the most extreme totalitarian state. Western man, who equates freedom with dignity, does not want to give up his freedom of choice, including the choice of whom he shall work for, unless it is truly necessary.

Many will argue that while this may be so, our manpower requirements make it a necessary evil to sacrifice a short time out of everyone's life. A professional army of present size, the generally accepted theory runs, is fiscally impossible. This is a completely untested theory, and in fact there is some strong evidence to the contrary. Examine the following news item:

> The new law [1967] also dismisses another alternative to the draft, the all-volunteer Army. Chief objection here is the cost. To make the pay and benefits attractive enough to replace draftees (and the estimated 40 per cent of enlistees who sign up primarily to escape being drafted), the Defense budget would have to be hugely increased. Pentagon estimates have ranged from $4.2 billion to as much as $17 billion a year.[37]

What do those figures mean? For one thing, if we divide the United States population by three, giving us an approximation of the number of family units in the United States, and divide that figure into the above estimates, we come up with estimates of $65 to $260 annually per family unit.[38] We find that the budget (with adjustment for the credibility gap) for fiscal 1968 is estimated, in August, 1967, to be $2,200 per family, while the portion of that allocated to the Department of Defense is estimated at about $1,300 per family unit. The increase that would then be necessary is only 3 to 12 per cent of the current estimated budget—expensive, yes, but far from the impossible task most people suspect. Perhaps it might be more desirable to tighten our belts a bit elsewhere. Certainly, for those who accept in whole or in part the earlier, more basic arguments against the draft, it is a possibility worth considering, particularly if the anti-draft sentiment gets worse.

---

[37] "Among Vietnam's Victims: The Draft," *Newsweek*, July 10, 1967, p. 43. Copyright, Newsweek Inc., July, 1967.

[38] All figures in this book are in 1967 dollars.

There is another possibility that might make the additional expenditures much less than even the lowest estimates. The military is divided currently into nine grades of enlisted men ranging from E-1 to E-9 which correspond to the ranks from private to sergeant (seaman to petty officer for the navy). The draft is of course used to supply the lower grades. A two-year man who maintains a clean service record is likely to be released as an E-4 (corporal), although he may be an E-3 (Pfc). A man who by choice serves over two years will probably be an E-4 as he enters his third year of service. At this pay grade of E-4 an important dividing line is encountered, as to both the willingness of men to serve and the availability of men to fill the pay grade. For grades above E-4 the situation differs sharply. Here the grades are filled mainly with career men; these men have generally "re-upped" (re-enlisted) at least once. This is summed up in the following chart:

GENERAL PAY STRUCTURE OF ENLISTED MEN IN
U.S. ARMY

E-1 through E-3	Men on their first enlistment, including draftees
E-4	Mixed
E-5 through E-9	Career men on at least their second enlistment

Of course, policies regarding promotion vary from time to time, base to base, unit to unit, depending on whether the serviceman is in the United States, overseas, in a combat zone, or in actual combat; nevertheless, this chart will serve as a general guide to an understanding of the "availability of labor" in the services and especially in the Army, where draftees are generally involved.

It is the E-5 through E-9 group with which we shall mainly concern ourselves. Here lies an enormous amount of dead weight —the bulk of the malcontents and ne'er-do-wells within the military. Most of those who we hear "couldn't make it in civilian life" fall within this group. There are alcoholics galore and men who, because they have not been caught, or do not ordinarily commit serious infractions of the Universal Code of Military Justice, or have worked their way up again since the last infraction, are given the equivalent of middle management positions—not on the strength of leadership ability or a particular skill valuable to the Army but rather because they have served sufficient "time in grade." Thus many become a burden both to the service and to the taxpayer. This is not to imply that all or even most NCO's are incompetent. On the contrary, there are tens of thousands who are excellent soldiers, leaders, and specialists within these ranks. This is especially true in the higher grades; few men make the rank of E-8 or E-9 without some merit. But the problem outlined does exist, and it is no small problem.

Since we need E-1's through E-3's and since we have too many of poor to average quality in the E-5 through E-7 group, the solution would be obvious to any large business organization. We should experiment by taking money away from the second group and offering it as an inducement to recruit more of the first group. But when Congress raises the pay of the Army, it usually does just the opposite. Often there is no pay raise for the lower grades—and no inducement for initial enlistment—while the pay of those likely to re-enlist is raised. Many of these latter men would remain in the Army for less money, for, as I pointed out, they like the military life, even though many don't contribute much to the military. So most pay increases passed by Congress merely serve to surfeit the already overcrowded pay grades. The military needs many less NCO's than it has and many more "yardbirds" than it is presently able to recruit from a free labor market.

This is not so harsh for the prospective career man as it may sound. There are many ways to reward the good soldier and there is no need to give anyone a pay cut. The military has used proficiency pay for quite a few years now. A soldier recommended by his commanding officer as above average in performance may be awarded a boost in pay over and above what the majority in his pay grade receive. It has its inequities, of course, as does promotion in business, but the concept is a large step forward. Tests for proficiency in whatever skills the soldier or other serviceman contributes to the service could be more widely used; or the answer might simply be a policy of promoting men on merit alone rather than on seniority (coupled with a big pay boost for what are now the lower enlisted grades). The "save pay" system would have to be utilized in any new pay law. This system has been used before in military pay changes. The term "save pay" means that no one will receive a pay cut. Only those men coming into the Army for the first time and those being promoted would be paid on the new pay scales. No one would receive less than he made at the time the new law went into effect. A soldier who had been busted, however, would, on working his way back up, have only his last pay grade considered. These specifics would of course have to be worked out by a congressional committee, and experimentation to find the proper balance would be important. But the concept as generally outlined should go a long way toward eliminating or at least substantially reducing the need for conscription in peacetime.

In this country Woodrow Wilson did everything in his power to keep us out of World War I. We were entering an age in which the Enlightenment was to fade into the background. Eastern ideas were creeping into Western society. The Eastern countries, Germany and Russia, had no Enlightenment. They went from serfdom and medieval society to totalitarianism. Society was becoming a machine and in many circles the old ideas were prematurely thought of as outmoded. The two world wars, the depression, and the cold war brought us propaganda, an outlook which placed the state in a more important position than ever before, and resulted in true loss of individualism. On the economic front policing was obviously necessary, but governments frequently became involved in unwise economic controls that aggravated matters rather than improved them. In America misunderstanding of money markets after the 1929–32 debacle brought many reforms that did not come near the heart of the problem. The so-called cold war became an excuse to go on an unrestrained spree of economic growth, at such a helter-skelter pace that it was bound to topple. The cold war was waged on the economic front in the name of a fictional competition with the USSR—a shameless American economic orgy. To buy Polish hams or Yugoslavian baskets became unpatriotic among the more extreme "patriots." During the fifties these chauvinists sometimes frowned on Americans who bought foreign cars made in Britain and other friendly nations. These same people would then bemoan the loss of individual freedom while doing everything they could to take it from the consumer. The value of trade as a tool to make unfriendly nations more friendly was completely lost on these people. (Consider, for instance, what might have been China's reaction had we offered our surplus wheat to her as a gesture of good will. Here would have been an example of true flower power. The mellowing effect might have been great.)

Wilson (as no doubt Thomas Jefferson would have been) was criticized for being too idealistic. On April 1, 1917, when he was nearly at his wit's end in his struggle to remain neutral in Europe, he spoke prophetic words about a nation that generally wished to remain at peace. He felt that if we entered the war, the world we knew would be overturned. If we upset the balance of neutrality, the world would be off a peace basis and onto a war basis. In anguish he told the editor of the New York *World:*

> Once lead this people into war and they'll forget there ever was such a thing as tolerance. To fight you must be brutal and ruthless, and the spirit of ruthless brutality will enter into the very fibre of our national life, infecting Congress, the courts, the policeman on the beat, the man in the street . . . If there is any alternative, for God's sake, let's take it.[39]

Wilson felt that freedom of speech and assembly could not survive the war and that the Constitution would crumble. He felt that no nation could put its full strength into an all-out war and keep its sanity. No nation had done it before.

---

[39] As quoted in Arthur S. Link, *Woodrow Wilson and the Progressive Era* (New York: Harper, 1954). The editor of the *World* was Frank Cobb.

He was right. Americans, who until 1917 had been essentially peace-loving people in spite of the unfortunate Spanish-American War incident, never got over the change that the twentieth century brought about. They ignored Wilson's pleas for the League of Nations and a reasonable peace settlement, not because they were war-weary and wanted once again to withdraw into their splendid isolationism, but because—

They were listening to something else. They were listening to ugly rumors of a huge radical conspiracy against the government and institutions of the United States. They had their ears cocked for the detonation of bombs and the tramp of Bolshevist armies. They seriously thought—or at least millions of them did, millions of otherwise reasonable citizens—that a Red revolution might begin in the United States the next month or next week, and they were less concerned with making the world safe for democracy than with making America safe for themselves.

Those were the days when column after column of the front pages of the newspapers shouted the news of strikes and anti-Bolshevist riots; when radicals shot down Armistice Day paraders in the streets of Centralia, Washington, and in revenge the patriotic citizenry took out of the jail a member of the I.W.W.—a white American, be it noted—and lynched him by tying a rope around his neck and throwing him off a bridge; when properly elected members of the Assembly of New York State were expelled (and their constituents thereby disfranchised) simply because they had been elected as members of the venerable Socialist Party; when a jury in Indiana took two minutes to acquit a man for shooting and killing an alien because he had shouted, "To hell with the United States"; and when the Vice-President of the nation cited as a dangerous manifestation of radicalism in the women's colleges the fact that the girl debaters of Radcliffe had upheld the affirmative in an inter-collegiate debate on the subject: "Resolved, that the recognition of labor unions by employees is essential to successful collective bargaining." It was an era of lawless and disorderly defense of law and order, of unconstitutional defense of the Constitution, of suspicion and civil conflict—in a very literal sense, a reign of terror.[40]

---

[40] Frederick Lewis Allen, *Only Yesterday* (New York: Harper, 1931), pp. 45-46.

This essentially irrational fear had some foundation. Attempts were made on the lives of a number of outstanding citizens, including cabinet members, by the device of bombs in the mails. These were thought to be the work of communists and anarchists. But then, as now, the troublemakers were a tremendously small minority, even within the Communist, Socialist, and Socialist Labor parties, which together comprised about one-tenth of one per cent of the adult population (according to Gordon S. Watkins, writing in the *Atlantic Monthly* in 1919).

But the American business man was in no mood to consider whether it was a slender nucleus or not. He, too, had come out of the war with his fighting blood up, ready to lick the next thing that stood in his way. He wanted to get back to business and enjoy his profits. Labor stood in his way and threatened his profits. He had come out of the war with a militant patriotism; and mingling his idealistic with his selfish motives, after the manner of all men at all times, he developed a fervent belief that 100-per-cent Americanism and the Welfare of God's Own Country and Loyalty to the Teachings of the Founding Fathers implied the right of the business man to kick the union organizer out of his workshop. He had come to distrust anything and everything that was foreign, and this radicalism he saw as the spawn of the long-haired Slavs and unwashed East-Side Jews. And, finally, he had been nourished during the war years upon stories of spies and plotters and international intrigue. He had been convinced that German sympathizers signaled to one another with lights from mountain-tops and put ground glass into surgical dressings, and he had formed the habit of expecting tennis courts to conceal gun-emplacements. His credulity had thus been stretched until he was quite ready to believe that a struggle of American laboring-men for better wages was the beginning of an armed rebellion directed by Lenin and Trotsky, and that behind every innocent professor who taught that there were arguments for as well as against socialism there was a bearded rascal from eastern Europe with a money bag in one hand and a smoking bomb in the other.[41]

When another bomb attempt killed the wrong man at Attorney General Palmer's home and a copy of a radical publica-

---

[41] *Ibid.*, pp. 48-49.

tion was found near his body, the American people reacted in a vicious, indiscriminate manner. The radical publication, so conveniently left at the scene of the crime, sounds like the type of thing critical readers of today's newspapers are all too familiar with. Nevertheless, there seemed to be a reasonable case that most of the outrages were the work of Reds. The growth of the Ku Klux Klan into a political force occurred during this period. The Sacco-Vanzetti case is one of the more notorious instances of what may have been a perversion of American justice due to galloping xenophobia. In a section that could be taken from a contemporary account, Allen continues:

> . . . For the professional super-patriot (and assorted special propagandists disguised as super-patriots) had only begun to fight. Innumerable patriotic societies had sprung up, each with its executive secretary, and executive secretaries must live, and therefore must conjure up new and ever greater menaces. Innumerable other gentlemen now discovered that they could defeat whatever they wanted to defeat by tarring it conspicuously with the Bolshevist brush. Big-navy men, believers in compulsory military service, drys, anti-cigarette campaigners, anti-evolution Fundamentalists, defenders of the moral order, book censors, Jew-haters, Negrohaters, landlords, manufacturers, utility executives, upholders of every sort of cause, good, bad, and indifferent, all wrapped themselves in Old Glory and the mantle of the Founding Fathers and allied their opponents with Lenin. The open shop, for example, became the "American plan." For years a pestilence of speakers and writers continued to afflict the country with tales of "sinister and subversive agitators." Elderly ladies in gilt chairs in ornate drawing-rooms heard from executive secretaries that the agents of the government had unearthed new radical conspiracies too fiendish to be divulged before the proper time. Their husbands were told at luncheon clubs that the colleges were honeycombed with Bolshevism. A cloud of suspicion hung in the air, and *intolerance became an American virtue.*[42] [Italics mine.]
>
> . . . Books, too, must be carefully scanned for the all-pervasive evil. Miss Hermine Schweid, speaking for the Better America

[42] *Ibid.*, pp. 58, 59.

Foundation, a band of California patriots, disapproved of [Sinclair Lewis's] *Main Street* because it "created a distaste for the conventional good life of the American."[43]

. . . His [Attorney General Palmer's] next move was to direct a series of raids in which Communist leaders were rounded up for deportation to Russia, *via* Finland, on the ship *Buford,* jocosely known as the "Soviet Ark." Again there was enthusiasm—and apparently there was little concern over the right of the Administration to tear from their families men who had as yet committed no crime. Mr. Palmer decided to give the American public more of the same; and thereupon he carried through a new series of raids which set a new record in American history for executive transgression of individual constitutional rights.

Under the drastic war-time Sedition Act, the Secretary of Labor had the power to deport aliens who were anarchists, or believed in or advocated the overthrow of the government by violence, or were affiliated with any organization that so believed or advocated. Mr. Palmer (the ailing Wilson's Attorney-General) now decided to "cooperate" with the Secretary of Labor by rounding up the alien membership of the Communist party for wholesale deportation. His under-cover agents had already worked their way into the organization. . . .[44]

In scores of cities all over the United States, when the Communists were simultaneously meeting at their various headquarters on New Year's Day of 1920, Mr. Palmer's agents and police and voluntary aides fell upon them—fell upon everybody, in fact, who was in the hall, regardless whether he was a Communist or not (how could one tell?)—and bundled them off to jail, with or without warrant. Every conceivable bit of evidence—literature, membership lists, books, papers, pictures on the wall, everything—was seized, with or without a search warrant. On this and succeeding nights other Communists and suspected Communists were seized in their homes. . . .[45]

. . . But at the time the newspapers were full of reports from Mr. Palmer's office that new evidence of a gigantic plot against the

---

[43] *Ibid.*, p. 60.
[44] *Ibid.*, p. 56.
[45] *Ibid.*, p. 57.

safety of the country had been unearthed; and although the steel strike was failing, the coal strike was failing, and any danger of a socialistic regime, to say nothing of a revolution, was daily fading, nevertheless to the great mass of the American people the Bolshevist bogey became more terrifying than ever.

Mr. Palmer was in full cry. In public statements he was reminding the twenty million owners of Liberty bonds and the nine million farm-owners and the eleven million owners of savings accounts, that the Reds proposed to take away all they had. He was distributing boiler-plate propaganda to the press, containing pictures of horrid-looking Bolsheviks with bristling beards, and asking if such as these should rule over America. Politicians were quoting the suggestion of Guy Empey that the proper implements for dealing with the Reds could be "found in any hardware store," or proclaiming, "My motto for the Reds is S.O.S.—ship or shoot. I believe we should place them all on a ship of stone, with sails of lead, and that their first stopping-place should be hell." College graduates were calling for the dismissal of professors suspected of radicalism; school-teachers were being made to sign oaths of allegiance; business men with unorthodox political or economic ideas were learning to hold their tongues if they wanted to hold their jobs. Hysteria had reached its height.[46]

Some of the less obvious comparisons between that day and this can now be noted. First, Americans in large numbers made the same mistake then that they are making today in fancying that the enemy is *only* bolshevism. The Senate refused to ratify the League of Nations charter in much the same way that reactionaries today advocate that we should withdraw from the United Nations. (It is conceivable that a situation could someday develop in which a nation might find it intolerable to remain in the United Nations, but no such situation has ever arisen with regard to the United States nor are there any indications of it in the foreseeable future.) In the 1920's blind fear of anything that smacked of communism extended to Germany, where Americans feared that the communists might gain control. (As we are seeing, such a possibility for Germany was as remote as for the United States.) When the National Socialists took over in 1933,

---

[46] *Ibid.*, pp. 57, 58.

most Americans heaved a sigh of relief—it was only Hitler! The press, both then and now, bears no small responsibility for the American myopia regarding communism and the enemies of democracy. Then as now there were responsible elements of the press; but if they became too vocal in pointing out the general fallacious thinking, they were discredited as "pink" and lost much of their influence. Most of all, it must be noted just to what extent our present problems are a result of wartime controls. The action by Attorney General Palmer in deporting United States citizens without due process of law was the result of carrying over wartime controls into peacetime. These counterrevolutionary measures, perhaps defensible in time of national emergency, such as a world war, became a permanent part of America. From the wartime economies sprang totalitarianism—a phenomenon which has yet to be defined in this work, but is not simply a dictatorship of Right or Left. Palmer and Colton's eloquent definition of totalitarianism follows:

> Totalitarianism was a many-sided thing. It had appeared first with the Bolshevik Revolution, for in the denial of individual liberty the Soviet regime did not differ from the most extreme anti-Soviet or fascist totalitarianism as manifested in Germany. . . .
>
> Totalitarianism, as distinct from mere dictatorship, though it appeared rather suddenly after the First World War, was no historic freak. It was an outgrowth of a good deal of development in the past. The state was an institution that had continuously acquired new powers ever since the Middle Ages; step by step, since feudal times, it had assumed jurisdiction over law courts and men at arms, imposed taxes, regulated churches, guided economic policy, operated school systems, and devised schemes of public welfare. The First World War had continued and advanced the process. The twentieth-century totalitarian state, mammoth and monolithic, claiming an absolute domination over every department of life, now carried this old development of state sovereignty to a new extreme. . . .
>
> This new philosophy drew heavily upon a historic nationalism which it greatly exaggerated. It derived in part from the organic theory of society, which held that society (or the nation or state) was a kind of living organism within which the individual person

was but a single cell. The individual, in this theory, had no independent existence; he received life itself, and all his ideas, from the society, people, nation, or culture into which he was born and by which he was nurtured. In Marxism, the absolute subordination of the individual to his class came to much the same thing. The individual was a microscopic cell, meaningless outside the social body. He was a little particle within a monolithic slab. He was but clay to be molded by the imprint of his group. It made little sense, given such theories, to speak of the individual's "reason" or "freedom," or to allow individuals to have their own opinions (which were formed for them by environment), or to count up individual opinions to obtain a merely numerical majority. Valid ideas were those of the group as a whole, of the people or nation (or, in Marxism, the class) as a solid block. Even science was a product of specific societies: there was a "Nazi science" which was bound to differ in its conclusions from democratic, bourgeois, Western, or "Jewish" science; and for the Soviets there was a Soviet science, consistent with dialectical materialism, and better equipped to see the truth than the decadent bourgeois, capitalistic or "fascist" science of the non-Soviet world. . . . The avowed philosophy of totalitarian regimes (like much modern thought) was basically subjective. Whether an idea was held to be true depended on whose idea it was. Ideas of truth, or beauty, or right were not supposed to correspond to any outer or objective reality; they had only to correspond to the inner nature, interests, or point of view of the people, nation, society, or class that entertained such ideas. The older concepts of reason, natural law, natural right, and the ultimate alikeness of all mankind, or of a common path of all mankind in one course of progress, disappeared.

The totalitarian regimes did not simply declare . . . that peoples' ideas were shaped by environment. They set about shaping them actively. Propaganda became a principal branch of government. Propaganda was hardly new; but in the past, and still in the democratic countries, it had been a piecemeal affair, urging the public to accept this or that political theory, or to buy this or that brand of coffee. Now, like all else, it became "total." Propaganda was monopolized by the state, and it demanded faith in a whole view of life and in every detail of this co-ordinated whole. Formerly the control of books and newspapers had been mainly negative; under Napoleon or Metternich, for example, censors had forbidden statements on particular subjects, events or persons. Now, in totalitarian countries, control of the press became frighteningly positive. The government manufactured thought. It manipulated opinion. It rewrote history. Writers were required to present whole ideologies, and books, newspapers, magazines, and the radio diffused an endless and overwhelming cloud of words. Loudspeakers blared in the streets, gigantic blown-up photographs of the Leader looked down in public places. . . .

The very idea of truth evaporated. No norm of human utterance remained except political expediency—the wishes and self-interest of the men in power. No one could learn anything except what the government wanted him to know. No one could escape the omnipresent official doctrine, the insidious penetration of the very recesses of his mind by ideas planted by outsiders for their own purposes. People came to accept, and even to believe, the most extravagant statements when they were endlessly repeated, year after year. Barred from all independent sources of information, having no means by which any official allegation could be tested, the peoples of totalitarian countries became increasingly in fact, and not merely in sociological theory, incapable of reason.

Violence, the acceptance and even glorification of violence, was indeed the characteristic most clearly distinguishing the totalitarian from the democratic systems . . . a cult of violence, or belief that struggle was beneficial, had arisen before the First World War. The war itself habituated people to violence and direct action. Lenin and his followers showed how a small group could seize the helm of state under revolutionary or chaotic conditions. Mussolini in 1922 taught the same lesson, with further refinements; for the Italy in which he seized power was not at war, and it was merely the threat or possibility of revolution, not revolution itself, that provided him with his opportunity. In the 1920's, for the first time since the seventeenth century, some of the most civilized parts of Europe, in time of peace, saw private armies marching about the country, bands of uniformed and organized ruffians, Blackshirts or Brownshirts, who manhandled, abused and even killed law-abiding citizens with impunity. Nor would anyone in the 1920's have believed that, by the 1930's, Europe would see the re-introduction of torture.[47]

---

[47] *Op. cit.*, pp. 811-15.

Here, then, is the enemy in full perspective with ghastly clarity. The tendency is all too obvious. Totalitarianism, the enemy of the Enlightenment, the counterrevolution to the American Revolution, the product of an extremism carried to previously unimaginable and frightening conclusions, is a product not only of the East but of the twentieth century. The trend toward subverting the individual to the state is as evident in the United States as elsewhere. People complain of such abstract things as losing their identity. (Imagine Thomas Jefferson and Benjamin Franklin making the same complaint.) Private armies, mostly of extreme philosophy, abound. Serious attempts are made to ban the tales of Robin Hood and other classics from the schools because they are supposedly socialistic. Propaganda, nearly a generation after the close of World War II, is still with us. So is a credibility gap, which is not much different. Class warfare, in the form of racial rioting, erupts. There are pressures to do away with such concepts of the Enlightenment as reason, natural law, and natural right. Our government attempts to manufacture thought in foreign affairs, economics, and any controversial policy it undertakes wholeheartedly. The Ku Klux Klan is still with us. Negroes and civil-rights workers are murdered in the South. Violence, the trademark of totalitarianism, rises on the domestic front to a degree not seen since the aftermath of the Civil War. The Jews rose in Germany in the area of economic competition; the Negro rises in America and competes with the white man for jobs. The beatnik, vietnik, and beard are tolerated in some places less than the Negro. Congressmen wish to throw "dirty, long-haired, Communist-led beatniks" overboard with their hands chained behind their backs, as they did forty-five years ago. (A deep sense of resentment, perhaps a "stab in the back" philosophy, could arise if we are forced out of Vietnam.) Hitler rose to power in the throes of depression; depression threatens the United States. The situation in this land may be much graver than is generally realized. A fascist takeover is even more fearsome to contemplate in a nuclear-armed nation.

It may surprise those who have read this far that I consider myself a conservative. True conservatism does not mean reaction.

It adopts the ideas of the previously mentioned Alcoholics Anonymous prayer, which asks for "wisdom to know the difference." As the British Conservative party does not continually try to hark back to the days of aristocracy (except in mere formality; e.g., Sir Ringo Starr), so American conservatives must learn to realize when a battle such as the one over social security or a progressive income tax has been lost. The role of the pragmatic conservative is to improve the present situation and to offer constructive suggestions. The conservative should be against wasteful spending in government, but he must be politic about it. He can work to retain laissez faire when practicable, without dogmatism. He must be willing to deviate from fixed positions when he senses a necessary and worthy cause. Above all, he must conserve the American Revolution.

I will now deviate for a moment from the language used throughout this book and honor those who have been harassed with the name *reactionary,* by applying the more honorable term *conservative,* if only in the vain hope that a few may have accepted some of the ideas forwarded here. Too much conservative thought, however, exclusively equates totalitarianism and communism, guarding the one door while leaving the rear entrance wide open. We are jumping into the very pit we are trying to avoid. In the long run no true American of any stripe would relish what might be created. The specter of violence, perhaps soon to be nourished by *major* economic problems, is in the air. Reason is a narrow road in a dense totalitarian forest. America is still looked upon in many, albeit diminishing, circles as the last chance for an Enlightened world. If we are to fulfill that hope, we must change our course. The purpose here is not to alienate conservatives from the American Revolution, as they have frequently alienated others for over forty-five years, but instead to make an updated appeal to those old-fashioned values of rationalism and reason. Before it is too late and if we still can, for God's sake let us reason together.

One of Wilson's most famous concepts, that of making the world safe for democracy, should be mentioned. This is another example of a great idea which has been perverted by the Dulleses and the Johnsons in the cold war. Current interpretations of this concept bear little resemblance to Wilson's original meaning. Making the world safe for democracy could and should provide a sensible foreign policy for America in the nuclear age. An allegiance with those countries whose government is rooted in the Enlightenment has nothing to do with fighting for a government that has no more of a true understanding of freedom than has its enemy, as in Vietnam. Nor should it include an invasion of Cuba, a country that like Vietnam knew much less freedom under the old regime than under the present one. To help secure democracy would seem to require a complete neutrality regarding the conflicts in countries where freedom and democracy have never existed. Making the world safe for democracy is not the same as making the governments of the world sympathetic to the government of the United States nor even making the rest of the world democratic. It entails only allying ourselves with those bona fide democracies that choose to reciprocate our allegiance. It requires some sort of understanding of where freedom exists if freedom is to be defended. An example of how the United States had completely lost Wilson's meaning and let the truly free world down came in June of 1967, when we were fighting a major war for a reactionary government in Vietnam and declaring (if only for a short while) neutrality in word, thought, and deed regarding Israel. It takes a realization that all countries that are not communistic are not necessarily our friends and may even be our deadly enemies, the Arab countries being a prime example. The enemy is all non-democratic regimes that would war against free countries. It must be understood that all governments that call themselves communistic are not necessarily a threat to freedom. The unbelievable phobia some Americans have toward communism—their black-or-white concept of the communist monolith—not only makes these people imagine enemies where there are none; they fail to recognize the enemy when he appears in other garb. These people are so blind as to classify Algeria and Greece as part of the free world. Making the world safe for democracy does not mean expansionism (which would make it unsafe); rather, it means a sound policy of defense.

The Russian Revolution, like the French, overlooked the necessity of specific goals. It could have been considered either successful or unsuccessful, depending on which side one happened to be on in the bloody civil war that accompanied it. It represented the overthrow of an intolerable, albeit progressing, system. Serfdom was not abolished in Russia until 1861 (when the United States was warring to abolish slavery). The late date indicates how far Russia was behind the rest of Europe. Upon overthrowing the intolerable regime, Russia emerged from her chaotic civil war in a state no better than before so far as individual freedom was concerned. As the decades passed she did make great economic strides and elevated the material position of the common man. She skipped the Enlightenment and in true romantic fashion subverted the individual entirely to the welfare of the state.

The worst thing about the Russian Revolution was the class warfare. They plundered and killed any and all who were even suspected of sympathies with the falling regime. The bourgeoisie, or middle class (made up of those who were neither common laborers nor intellectuals), were slaughtered along with any who were sympathetic to them. Thus there emerged a regime built upon hate. In destroying so many indiscriminately, they unnecessarily destroyed the backbone of their society. Physicians, attorneys, and other professional men were virtually eliminated. Anyone with property, regardless of how he had used it or what his political sympathies had been, was marked as an enemy of the regime. Like the French in 1789, and like the American Negro with his riots today, they thrashed about in a class warfare which virtually annihilated their very environment.

It is said by the Chinese that some American Negroes are accepting Mao's teachings in becoming involved in class warfare. American newsmen counter that this is a Chinese perversion of an American phenomenon. But the Chinese seem to be essentially correct here. American Negroes in great numbers have declared an unfortunate class war. The surprising thing, at least until one understands the complete degradation that American slavery forced upon the Negro, is that this phenomenon did not happen earlier. But class warfare, especially against nine-to-one odds, is to no avail. The problem is that it is indiscriminate. The Negro is right, of course, in that a completely unprejudiced white, except among the New Left and the true hipsters, is an extreme rarity; it is therefore easy for the Negro to hate all whites indiscriminately. But the extreme tactical error remains. Racial prejudice is based on fear. Southern whites in particular even preserve the Freudian-tinted myth that if one of "their women" went to bed with a Negro, she would never again be satisfied with a man of her own race. To provide a *real* basis for fear in the form of class warfare is a mistake that it is understandable for the uneducated or non-thinking Negro to make. But for those in the Negro race who are otherwise clear-thinking, pragmatic men, it is hard to understand how they can feel that declaring an indiscriminate class war on *all* whites, including their small but fast-growing number of white friends, can further their cause. For the unprejudiced white, class warfare tends to cause aloofness; that is, he may begin to feel that however much he sympathizes and even identifies with the Negro cause, if the Negro declares war on him he must defend himself and his environment with no sense of responsibility for the actions of the mass of white bigots (whom our unprejudiced white dislikes just as much as does the Negro). The redneck, in turn, hates this unprejudiced white man; there is no more venomous hatred than that of many white southerners toward the white civil-rights worker. However, just as the white who is sympathetic to the Negro cause begins to support the cause of law and order he hears of police tearing up Negro-owned businesses, or committing other similar acts; and he may rather covertly and ironically begin to wish that the whole damned bunch of hate-filled bastards would end up killing each other off. Thus the white backlash extends to liberals too. In the true meaning of John Locke, the liberal cannot support the indiscriminate destruction of life and property. Discriminate war—yes! Indiscriminate war, class war, and senseless vandalism, however understandable—no!

He may feel, along with reactionaries, that the country must not reward a Negro community that has recently rioted, for that will only encourage others to riot. He may vote against anti-poverty funds because he feels that if the bill passed it may be regarded as having been passed under duress. The riots are the same type of tactical error as the attempted murder of government officials by means of bombs in the mails in 1919 (see pp. 121–22 above). It is up to moderate Negroes to help abort such tactics if they would further the cause of civil rights.

I will not go into detail about the Weimar Republic in Germany and why it failed. References have been made to that government throughout the text and the reader will already have some notion of the mistakes that were made. It will suffice to reiterate here that many of the errors made by German Liberals in the nineteenth century in tolerating reaction in the schools and other areas of society were made again. The Weimar Republic was not completely innocent of dictatorial tactics. Article 48 of the Weimar Constitution gave the president of the Republic the power to suspend the Constitution temporarily in order to restore order when sudden disturbances threatened the public safety. During the period from 1919 to 1932 this article was invoked no fewer than 250 times.[48] During the period of the Republic, excluding the final Nazi takeover, there were a few serious uprisings from both Left and Right, the most notable being the reactionary Kapp Putsch of 1920. The abuse of this provision, which reached its height under Paul von Hindenburg in the immediate period before Hitler, is evident from the fact that the article was invoked, on the average, every nineteen days. In invoking it, the German government never attacked the root of the problem—the basic reactionary attitude of the German people to the democracy.

The forcible rooting out of reactionary and totalitarian thought in education obviously runs the danger of becoming

---

[48] Clinton Rossiter, *Constitutional Dictatorship: Crisis Government in the Modern Democracies*, Harbinger ed. (New York: Harcourt, Brace & World), p. 33.

totalitarian itself. It presents a serious, but necessary, problem for a Liberal regime. One element to be avoided here is any trace of a leadership cult. Any official connection of the head of government or the system of government itself with right and wrong is to be avoided. The less government pervades society in unnecessary areas, the easier will be the task of the educator in instilling true respect for democratic government.

Finally we arrive at the present day in our historical narrative. A people who never really ridded themselves of the emergency measures of war economies found themselves suddenly in the nuclear age. The great depression of the 1930's presented us with a greatly magnified poverty problem that required emergency relief. With the experience of World War I still fresh in our minds, we expanded government control of the economic system on a broad base. This was unnecessary and an inefficient approach to the problem of poverty, which never left the American scene to any extent. Freedom of economic choice was inhibited. (This is not to advocate economic anarchy; the consumer must be protected. Economic freedom, like all freedom, requires responsibility.) Government became concerned with making the majority happy to the extent of promoting luxury rather than resolving their primary responsibility—poverty. Most New Deal programs dealt not with the permanent lower economic elements of society but mainly with those only temporarily out of money. The New Deal proved to be a stopgap program. FDR was no doubt sincere, in spite of his critics. But he was "economically illiterate." Nor did he know the money markets, although he lulled the American people into a false sense of security with the idea that "it can't happen again." He was a great President because of his concern for the impoverished and miserable, and his preservation of the capitalistic system by his defiance of many shortsighted capitalists. But the inefficiencies of a bureaucracy which attacked symptoms instead of the problem of poverty itself did nothing to preserve the Enlightenment, rid our nation of the wartime emergency system, or reverse the trend toward government control.

The nuclear age brought with it fear on a previously unimaginable level. As FDR said in a different context, fear was what we had to fear. Fear lessened our ability to compromise. Everyone, however unsophisticated, had his own formula for survival, usually rooted in pre-nuclear times. Fear breeds hatred and violence. Eisenhower reassured us in the Dulles era. Kennedy provided true relief from much of the danger. When he was shot down, we all saw how tenuous that apparent safety could be. This is our problem today.

PART THREE

Possible Solutions

In the last section I harshly criticized many aspects of American government and society. It is now time to offer some constructive alternatives. Let us first examine the racial disorders that are plaguing our nation at this time. The problem must be examined with the following in mind: (1) The primary goal is to avoid racial warfare, increase of class hatred, and further breaches of the peace. (2) This should be done without losing our concern about poverty and human dignity, yet without rewarding rioters. (3) The problem should also be attacked without losing sight of the goal of fiscal responsibility in government.

First, it must be realized just what the current class warfare constitutes. The race riots of the 1960's are outside the concept of sensible revolution as outlined in this book. For the Negro revolution to be successful, it must have specific goals in mind. Unless the American Negro knows what he is fighting for, either in the streets or in Congress, the revolution simply becomes a blind, senseless flailing. Goals cannot be achieved if no goals are stated. Secondly, after the goals are established, the means to achieve them must be agreed upon. The key here is discipline. However objectionable it may seem to some Negroes to have to cooperate with the white community, it must be realized that their goals can best be accomplished by joining forces with the much maligned white liberal in order to broaden the Negroes' basic strength. Discrimination does not always overrule violence.

It would be a direct attack on the enemy, for instance, to machine-gun a Ku Klux Klan meeting. By the same token, to indiscriminately pillage a white neighborhood would involve attacking many friends, even though a majority of those killed would be guilty of bigotry in some degree or other. At a KKK meeting there are no friends. In a cross section of American whites, there will be a handful just as hip as anyone and a great number of liberals who, however phony, are the best allies for advancement.

It is even more senseless to destroy one's own environment. Certainly that environment is often not what it should be, but destruction of private property is not helping matters in the least, especially when much of that property belongs to other Negroes. The primary role of government, as espoused by Locke, is the protection of property, including lives, from mankind in the "state of nature." The soul brother has as much right to expect the government to protect his home from being destroyed as does the white man. Thus, to destroy a fellow Negro's home or store harms the cause of civil rights by placing that Negro home owner or store owner outside the very purpose of government under the Enlightenment. The goal of a revolution, as Edmund Burke would say, is not to destroy your friends or their property—it is to destroy the enemy. If the property of a blood brother is not safe, then every advance the Negro has made in achieving equal rights under the law has been destroyed. The same is true of the white merchant. With obvious exceptions, the white people who express faith in the Negro community by investing what may be their life savings in that community are very likely to be the least bigoted of American whites. To destroy their confidence by burning and looting is to destroy a useful friendship. It will be economically impossible for many Negro communities to replace the homes and businesses which provide jobs and consumer services for years to come, if only because of high insurance rates. It is hardly a show of respect to the Negro majority to cause them such unnecessary problems.

It would seem that the best approach to attack the entire

problem of civil rights, protect life and property, and eliminate causes of dissatisfaction, while not rewarding communities that have rioted, is to keep the problems separate. The foremost goal of the government should be to maintain the peace. For instance, a federal grant of $80,000,000 (in 1967 dollars) to beef up the Detroit police force's riot control would not be too much. Rioters should and must be prosecuted to the fullest extent of the law. Looting a store of a refrigerator is grand larceny, the same as if the theft had occurred during a riot or in more peaceful times. If the jails of the country must be expanded, then let them be. In order to avoid the indiscriminate brutalizing of innocent by-standers, as has occurred all too often in the past, the federal grant might go toward a school for riot control, with stress on discipline of the police. The law-enforcement agencies must be strong and well trained to tackle any reasonable contingency effectively. And the community should not be rewarded with federal grants to help it rebuild what it has destroyed. No new, additional programs, with the exception of educational programs, should be initiated for a community that has recently rioted. The government should not legislate social progress under threat of duress. Innocent property owners who cannot collect from insurance companies would, unfortunately, have to suffer the consequences. (The government is not in the insurance business.) In this way, the problem of riots could be handled with color-blind equality. If white people tear up their community, the government must respond in the same manner as if they were black. By treating this as a problem of law enforcement rather than a problem of race, the government can remain officially color-blind. Indulgence by the government can only lead to more class warfare in the end. If the government does not act firmly to preserve the peace, and if it does not remain officially color-blind, then the white backlash could take on aspects similar to what we have seen in German racism.

This approach need not ignore the basic problems. Color blindness does not imply that civil-rights legislation need be ignored. Civil-rights legislation is in itself color-blind, at least in wording if not in application. Open-housing ordinances and other needed civil-rights acts must still be passed and enforced, for we are keeping the riots separate, in our minds, from the civil-rights movement. This is as it should be, for the riots have no part in the movement of moderate Negro leaders.

Poverty, then, should be attacked by an entirely new approach. We have built up a mishmash of inefficient bureaucratic programs which attack the symptoms rather than the root of poverty. Programs initiated for Watts have hardly scratched the surface. The inefficiencies are the natural result of the history of economic liberalism in this nation as well as in other Western democracies. First, the liberals, realizing that they can get only a little bit at a time, manage to pass a program—perhaps social security—over the objections of conservatives. The act, to a minor extent, takes care of the problem of poverty for elderly people—a small percentage of the population; the vast major portion of poverty remains. Next, some unemployment benefits may be passed in the same manner, helping some of the unemployed with generally inadequate benefits, but leaving many—those who are just entering the labor market, those whose benefits have expired, and endless others—outside the program. So it goes through a vast array of ideas and legislation, including job corps, slum-clearance and model-cities programs, WPA projects, farm subsidies, ad infinitum, with thousands of programs overlapping under hundreds of departments, agencies, and commissions. This often leaves out the most needy because of the limitations of the specific programs. This is the valid complaint of the conservative, but the inefficiencies generated should be the concern of the liberal as well. Yet, as was pointed out earlier, the Declaration of Independence itself implies it is the responsibility of the nation to guarantee the necessities of life to everyone, if at all possible. We are not concerned with the government's providing luxuries. As the British conservative (whose approach should be studied by the American conservative) tries to improve and streamline the hodgepodge Labour programs and seems to have no trouble in recognizing when a major battle has been lost—such as election reform, slavery, or the National Health Service (socialized medicine)—the major task of en-

lightened conservatives should be to offer an efficient, stream-
lined approach to the economic problems besetting the nation.

I would be in favor of ridding ourselves of virtually all government subsidy programs and substituting a guaranteed annual
wage (GAW)—probably, for the sake of administrative efficiency,
in the form of a reverse income tax. This would be especially
desirable with regard to riots in that a community would not be
directly rewarded for rioting under such a program, yet individuals really in need would be aided. The GAW would be automatic and impersonal with regard to race, individual, and community. It would solve the basic economic cause of riots. It
would have to be realistic. A single individual needs somewhere
around $1,400 a year to live decently in most communities in this
country. This figure easily supplies him with the necessities of
life—adequate quarters, food, clothing, cigarettes, an occasional
movie. A couple needs not quite double this amount, but very
nearly. There must, of course, be no upper limit to the number of
dependents the taxpayer or recipient is able to claim. If he supports twenty children and a wife, he must have adequate money
for twenty-two people. There are, in fact, realistic tables along
these lines already in existence which are utilized as poverty
guides in the Office of Economic Opportunity.

This proposal should go very deep. In a major codification
such as this, social security could be eliminated. It is already
ridiculous to take social-security benefits out of a separate tax
fund rather than from the general fund—a glaring example of the
inefficiencies of our system. Social security would thus be improved. Those who needed the benefits would receive more,
and those who preferred to continue their productive life could
do so much more easily. Those who did not need the benefits
would be cut out—another advantage. By providing a basic
wealth for the community as a whole, such projects as slum
clearance could then be shifted to state and local governments.
Tax-money spending would no longer be concentrated on raising
middle-class economic standards, and a great step toward providing the "natural" elimination of slums would evolve. Heads
of households who misused the privileges gained by spending

their monthly checks at the local tavern would be responsible to the laws of non-support in the same manner as any other member of society. There is no reason to suppose that such a streamlining of economic benefits would create any major problem in individual initiative. This is the basic reason for confining the benefits to a decent subsistence level. Most people want more. But it is our responsibility only to provide them with a fundamental base. This can be done within the limits of fiscal responsibility by ridding ourselves of the existing inefficient and inadequate programs.

Another advantage, and perhaps the major one, is that the GAW would provide us with an *automatic* two-sided Keynesian base. That is, in periods of depression the government would pay out more, and when the economy was working well, the government would take in more money to slow down a growth rate that might again become overheated, while stockpiling funds for the next downward dip in the business cycle. Most individuals would probably pay money to the government in taxes during most of the years of their productive lives and have occasion to draw from the government for perhaps a couple of years.

During the New Deal there was a feeling in the administration that outright relief was somehow degrading (hence the WPA, CCC, and other inefficient programs). This is sheer Victorian nonsense. There can be dignity in poverty; the indignity is found only when one is satisfied to remain impoverished. Perhaps by coupling relief with the income-tax system, into which one has paid or will pay for most of his life, this archaic attitude can be eliminated. Who would feel degraded taking money from an Internal Revenue Service fund in an emergency after having contributed a good percentage of his earnings over a varying period of time? Certainly no one should feel embarrassed by such a dole, any more than by a social-security check or a conventional tax refund. An occasional established program would have to be maintained. It is hard to see, for instance, how we can afford to cut our educational outlays. Instead, a person of productive age might receive his GAW only if he is taking advantage of an opportunity to advance himself. An individual example will illustrate: A former neighbor of mine with an eighth-grade education fell off a roof on his construction job and permanently injured his leg to the extent that he could never perform normal manual labor again. This man, who had a wife and two children, drew a disability pension which was to expire a year after the accident. During the first year of disability, his wife supplemented the family income at very low wages by working at the soda fountain of a drugstore. The injured man never really admitted to himself that he couldn't do construction work again, but he was fond of pointing out that he had no education and thus while he was "recuperating" could not do much of anything else. He felt there were no job opportunities available. During that year, which he spent generally fishing and watching TV, the local high school just a block away was offering adult-education courses in bookkeeping and typing, and general courses for high-school diplomas. There was nothing whatever wrong with the man's intelligence: he was capable of a doctorate had he been so inclined. Needless to say, at the end of that year when reality had to be faced, the man was in an economic bind he could have avoided.

One's failure to receive an advanced education has in recent years been largely a matter of choice in this country. To have things work smoothly, a society consisting of relatively few educated people and a large mass of laborers is needed. But the opportunities have been generally open to all, and this is as it should be, regardless of family or economic status. Average intelligence is capable of the highest academic goals; only the truly feeble-minded are at a disadvantage. Academic advancement is generally a matter of how one applies himself rather than of differences in potential. Today one's academic level is more a matter of cultural choice than anything else. A youth determined to rise above a hillbilly environment, for instance, can go to college by saving during summer work, working part time during the school term, washing dishes for his meals, applying for loans and possibly scholarships that are available, and utilizing the many excellent state institutions where tuition is quite reasonable or virtually nonexistent. (At many state institutions, how-

ever, the trend, during this cold-war boom, has been toward more
expensive education. At Indiana University tuition has risen a
sharp 175 per cent in fourteen years, and is due for another
hike immediately, while the cost of living in the country generally increased less than 30 per cent during the same period.
This would seem to indicate that the people of Indiana have
not kept up in the field of education. To a great extent this is
the fault of the university itself. There is an unfortunate general
trend toward Pepsi-generation luxury in the university—an over-
expansion not directly connected with quality or quantity of
education. Luxury apartments are made available to married
students for as high as $165 a month and at the same time there
is no low-cost housing available except a few old Army barracks
in the process of being torn down, for which there is a long wait-
ing list. This philosophy extends throughout the entire university
in its expansion program and is all too prevalent on other cam-
puses. At Indiana the cost of housing has gone up accordingly
in the past ten years over the entire city of Bloomington, mostly
because of the university's failure to provide low-cost student
housing.)

An example of a program which should be eliminated forth-
with rather than on a "save pay" basis is the farm subsidy program. This is because of the obvious difference in the nature
of the government's pledge to the recipient as opposed to veterans' benefits or social security. It might be desirable, however, to eliminate the program over a period of time, *no longer*
than ten years. And of course the government must complete
existing commitments. The problem here is the excessive number of lobbying interests that will want similar exceptions or
gradual leveling-off periods for their particular subsidies. Veterans' benefits, except for disabled veterans, should also be
largely elimniated. This does not indicate any lack of appreciation for the sacrifice of the veteran; but, rather, a substantial
portion of the savings might go toward a more direct display of
that appreciation by giving the serviceman more money while
he's actually serving and by further taking pressure off the draft.
The GI bill, which is money well spent by the country in raising

its educational standards, could be channeled into education for the public in general in order to give equal opportunity to the poor 4-F.

Among the most unfortunate government subsidies are the FHA program and similar programs designed to subsidize home ownership. Besides the usual disadvantages, such programs tend to make labor immobile, creating an unfortunate inflexibility in the economy.

Most important of all, the system of a guaranteed annual wage in lieu of the existing bureaucracy would hark back to basic respect for the individual. It would presume that Americans, poor as well as rich, have the basic common sense to spend their money in their own best interests. It would bring a bit of laissez faire into the general area of public welfare and thus represent a compromise for all concerned. A few would not handle their money wisely, as we all know. But to conclude from this that individual initiative and choice has failed in general is no more valid than to conclude that because of our present bureaucratic mess public welfare in general has failed. It is contrary to the ideas of Locke and Jefferson to presume that the individual American cannot run his own life. While an attitude of laissez faire must not be carried to an extreme, an attitude similar to laissez faire must remain the basic social philosophy of the government regarding the individual.

The twentieth century is too materialistically oriented. The government must eliminate poverty, but must not eliminate the bottom of the business cycle (an elimination which is proving disastrous). The government could better concern itself with the happiness of the people by directly attacking poverty instead of, as currently, making roundabout attempts to influence employment. We have recently found that when unemployment gets too low (generally less than 5 per cent), inflation gets too high. It seems that our problem has been misdiagnosed. The basis of our current system has been a concern not with poverty but with an average income and an uninterrupted growth rate in a race with the Soviet Union. The race has been unnecessary because of our commanding lead, and the policy of an uninterrupted growth rate created a catastrophe. Let us take care of our poor, whether temporarily or permanently poor, and make our system a bit less complicated so that it is not so hard to police.

The proposal above has not touched upon an important necessity—medical attention for the poor. Most pragmatists will not care whether we have socialized medicine or not. The main concern is that no one go without medical attention when he need it. There is nothing philosophically objectionable in socialized medicine within the framework of pragmatic conservatism as it has been outlined; however, there is a reasonable alternative for compromise for those who do object to the idea, if they wish to save the present system. Simply stated, no one would be questioned about his ability to pay upon entering a physician's office or hospital. If, upon *leaving* the medical facility, he felt he was unable to pay, he would then ask for the proper government application. As soon as the federal agency received the application, the obligation to the physician, clinic, or hospital would be recorded, and a monthly check meeting any such obligation sent without question (provided it was within liberally reasonable price standards, generally in line with the charge to patients not receiving government aid). The applications of the patients, however, would be spot-checked for fraud, in the same manner that income-tax returns are checked, in line with a government-established guideline for such medical care. As a matter of fact, the applications for medical help could probably best be handled by expanding the Internal Revenue Service so that it would be an easy matter to compare the applications against tax returns. If this reasonable compromise were proposed by the AMA, it would probably end all serious agitation for further socialization of medicine.

All of these programs would be opposed by people adversely affected by the change. Insurance companies might lobby against the medical-aid proposal (but not necessarily because the proposal would be to their advantage in the long run). Farmers would want to save their subsidies, veterans' organizations would want to save the subsidies of their members, and government employees would protest the elimination of unnecessary jobs. The taxpayer and citizen, however, should find such a major overhaul greatly to his advantage, and that affects us all. We have seen that in spite of our being the wealthiest nation on earth, the present system does not eliminate poverty; and we can now see that conservative concern with fiscal responsibility was not entirely wrong. With a possible depression and a domestic crisis, as well as a permanent foreign-policy crisis on our hands, major overhauls are imperative if we are to survive.

Another area to which there is no philosophical objection, as I interpret Locke, is the nationalization of utilities and of public transportation. All these services come easily under the concept of public utility (although heavy industry, such as steel, probably does not fall within the concept). This is not, however, a proposal to nationalize the telephone companies and the airlines: the necessity of nationalization would have to be demonstrated for each individual industry. American Telephone is in fact advancing at such a tremendous pace that it is hard to imagine any government agency being able to do as well, and its rates are well regulated by the FCC. Bus service is too expensive, however. There should be a means of cheap public transportation available, as in Mexico where one can ride a bus for about an American cent a mile. The shortage of passenger train service is an inconvenience, but the railroads have discontinued the service with government permission, so the railroads themselves are not to blame. Such problems for the consumer can be solved through either government subsidy and regulation or outright nationalization, preferably whichever appears to be substantially cheaper for the taxpayer.

These transportation problems do not seem to be serious problems to the nation at the moment. But it is hoped that conservatives will be able to accept the idea that these are reasonable areas for compromise and negotiation. No industry, of course, should ever be nationalized without reasonable reimbursement to the stockholders.

The most important area which is sorely in need of fresh ideas is foreign affairs. Each country during any given period in its history tends to be characterized with highly nebulous and debatable national traits. This is also true of its foreign policy. We classify the Italians as excitable, and we think of the Germans as a nation of beer-drinking, fun-loving, obedient, clumsy scientists and soldiers. The British are often thought of as conservative or as a nation of shopkeepers. We think of the Danes as easygoing and the French as a blindly nationalistic, volatile people who are likely to panic at the first sign of a major fight unless they are sure of their ability to come out on top. National character such as this is obviously imprecise, just as it is imprecise to think of all Americans as wearing a ten-gallon hat and outbidding all competition for the B-girl of his choice at a bar on the French Riviera while buying a round for the house and over-tipping the bartender. A nation's foreign policies, too, while also quite volatile, nevertheless develop characteristics which scholars, statesmen, and diplomats attempt to describe as typical of that nation for long periods of time.

The British are also thought of as having a shopkeeper philosophy in foreign affairs. The French are said to be fickle. The Germans are characterized with a certain unwarranted paranoia, as we have seen. The one word *always* used to describe American foreign policy is *moralistic*. The traditional policy of the British, especially in the nineteenth century, has been pragmatic. They would enter a war to protect British trading interests or the freedom of the seas. They would risk a larger war when their position as the major maritime power or when the European power balance was threatened. If their national existence was endangered, they would fight to the very end if need be, but as soon as the issue was decided in their favor, there was generally no thought of carrying it further by trying to conquer or meddle in the internal affairs of the conquered nation. The United States, however, has never been able to involve herself in any kind of war without first arousing herself to such a pitch of moralistic fervor that the war took on aspects of a holy crusade. Woodrow Wilson and the American people remained aloof from the great European conflict until 1917, preaching reasonableness and light and "peace without victory"—an honorable settlement for van-

quished and victors alike. But when the United States did find
it necessary to enter the war, the press worked up the American
people into a high state. Even Wilson himself, on addressing
Congress, lost that sweet reasonableness. Moral issues were at
stake. The Kaiser was the devil incarnate. The goal of a reasonable peace temporarily disappeared from the President's
speeches. Kennan discusses the United States entry into the war:

> Once in the war, we had no difficulty in discovering—and lost no
> time in doing so—that the issues involved in it were of the great-
> est significance to us.
>
> It is surely a curious characteristic of democracy: this amazing
> ability to shift gears overnight in one's ideological attitudes, de-
> pending on whether one considers one's self at war or at peace.
> Day before yesterday, let us say, the issues at stake between our-
> selves and another power were not worth the life of a single
> American boy. Today, nothing else counts at all; our cause is
> holy; the cost is no consideration; violence must know no limita-
> tions short of unconditional surrender.
>
> Now I know the answer to this one. A democracy is peace-
> loving. It does not like to go to war. It is slow to rise to provoca-
> tion. When it has once been provoked to the point where it must
> grasp the sword, it does not easily forgive its adversary for having
> produced the situation. The fact of the provocation then becomes
> itself the issue. Democracy fights in anger—it fights for the very
> reason that it was forced to go to war. It fights to punish the
> power that was rash enough and hostile enough to provoke it—
> to teach that power a lesson it will not forget, to prevent the thing
> from happening again. Such a war must be carried to the bitter
> end.
>
> This is true enough, and if nations could afford to operate in
> the moral climate of individual ethics, it would be understandable
> and acceptable. But I sometimes wonder whether in this respect
> a democracy is not uncomfortably similar to one of those pre-
> historic monsters with a body as long as this room and a brain the
> size of a pin: he lies there in his comfortable primeval mud and
> pays little attention to his environment; he is slow to wrath—in
> fact, you practically have to whack his tail off to make him aware
> that his interests are being disturbed; but once he grasps this,
> he lays about him with such blind determination that he not only

destroys his adversary but largely wrecks his native habitat. You wonder whether it would not have been wiser for him to have taken a little more interest in what was going on at an earlier date and to have seen whether he could not have prevented some of these situations from arising instead of proceeding from an undiscriminating indifference to a holy wrath equally undiscriminating.[1]

We all know what happened once we were at war. Victory must be total! Surrender must be unconditional! Never mind that America's best interests might lie in a European power balance or in a Germany which would not feel that the peace forced upon her was a *diktat*. But Kennan is not really describing a democracy—he is describing the United States. For Britain is a democracy, and as we have noted, Britain's foreign policy has never been based on isolationism, like that of the prehistoric monster just described. Whether Kennan's monster actually existed is an academic question; but if it did, perhaps some fate put that creature on earth in order to illustrate United States isolationism before World War II. But in another way Kennan is also describing all the Western democracies in the twentieth century. As we have noted, the wartime governments in the world wars all propagandized against the enemy in order to make the allied cause seem holy.

In the nuclear age, America, armed with the most fearsome weapons, took over the job of policing the world from Great Britain. On the other side stood the Soviet Union of Joseph Stalin, steeped in an ideology of class warfare and led by a pragmatic, amoral leader who used his power to grab every piece of territory and concession that he could. Stalin gave substance to the Big Red Scare by controlling other communist nations with force so that the communist bloc was truly monolithic. The situation, of course, was bound to be temporary, created as it was by

---

[1] Reprinted from *American Diplomacy, 1900-1950*, by George F. Kennan, pp. 65-66, by permission of the University of Chicago Press. Copyright 1951 by the University of Chicago. All rights reserved. Copyright 1951 under the International Copyright Union. Published 1951. Composed and printed by the University of Chicago Press, Chicago, Illinois, U.S.A.

the exigencies of World War II. Upon Stalin's death in March, 1953, the monolith gradually began to splinter, a process which had been presaged by Tito's rebellion in Yugoslavia. But by now the United States was well into the age of McCarthyism, and Dulles was entering the picture. Traditional American moralism was again reaching an irrational height—this time with the United States armed with nuclear bombs. Our isolationism no longer existed. In its place was a country and a State Department which confirmed the accusations of immaturity that were heaped upon us. Communism was "godless" and therefore we were right. The *free world* came to mean not democratic but capitalist. Thus Saudi Arabia and even Haiti became part of the free world. The free world became as monolithic in the minds of Americans as the communist world. Neutralist nations and allies alike who disagreed with us on the slightest detail were "disloyal," or their governments were "pink." The Dulles policy was to demand obedience from the "free world" as the USSR had from the communist world. In 1954, when the French lost Indochina, Admiral Arthur Radford said that Indochina must not be allowed to fall into communist hands lest such a fate set in motion a "falling row of dominoes."[2] This phrase was quickly echoed by Vice-President Nixon, Dulles, and then Eisenhower. Any neutral observer unaware of the ideological hysteria involved would at least seriously question the domino theory after a quick glance at a world map. Without admitting that the nuclear age had ushered in any profound change in warfare, Dulles pursued a policy similar to Stalin's—a policy of brinkmanship, or seeing how far we could go without the Soviet Union's pushing the nuclear trigger. War was to be all or nothing. No adjustment was to be made if the issues involved did not actually involve democracy's survival. If we felt it was right, then we were prepared to back it up with our entire nuclear arsenal. Dulles, the son of a Presbyterian minister, was prepared to invoke God and the entire United States war machine, it seemed, any time we did not get our way. Fortunately for the world, Stalin was dead. Two

[2] Chalmer M. Roberts, "The Day We Didn't Go to War," *The Reporter*, Sept. 14, 1954.

superpowers utilizing Stalin's tactics might have been too much. The United States at this time was a bigger threat to world peace than the Soviet Union. (Marx had fully expected that communism would emerge as a monolithic force. Indeed, Stalin's Bismarckian abilities to hold the communist bloc together made it appear for a while as if this was so. But upon the death of Stalin, nationalism began to emerge in the communist countries. The myth of the monolith, however, continues in official United States policy right through the Johnson-Rusk administration. Thus we have the strange spectacle of the United States government accepting a Marxian error while the communist countries do not.)

Under President Kennedy there was a short period of respite and progress. Kennedy made a serious mistake in allowing the Bay of Pigs fiasco to start at all, but the rest of his administration was generally free from moralistic rocket-rattling in foreign affairs. The 1962 missile crisis had nothing to do with ideology but rather was a question of national security. Great strides were made during Kennedy's administration to ease the cold war. Rusk and McNamara seemed willing allies in this endeavor. We had apparently reached the end of dangerous moralism in foreign policy. But after Kennedy's death, although European tensions relaxed, we embarked upon the massive acceleration in Vietnam.

So we succeeded in making the world unsafe for democracy. To make the world safe for democracy we should not choose sides in fights between non-democratic countries. We must understand that such a country as Chile is fully democratic with its Social Democratic president. Democracy is not an economic system. It is the way of free men to choose from among negotiable alternatives in economics just as in any other area. We cannot defend the Trujillos, the Duvaliers, and the Imans of Yemen and still live up to our professed goals. As Americans who want to make the world safe for democracy, we must support the Enlightenment in foreign affairs. We must take care not to make again the mistake that we made in Cuba—driving the government of that country into an unfriendly camp because of our own intransigence. Cuba could have been a great friend of the United States if only we had not tried to concern ourselves with the manner in which she chose to attack her domestic problems. A fairly realistic proposal would seem to be to pledge ourselves to defend, to the best of our capabilities (provided our aid was wanted), the true democracies—Europe west of the Communist line and excluding Iberia and Greece; Israel; the British Commonwealth; perhaps Japan and the Philippines if the democratic governments there can maintain internal control *without our aid;* and those Latin-American countries which are true democracies. In other countries we would remain neutral until a nation arrived at a truly Enlightened government upon its own. Then we could offer our protection to that government, while at the same time being prepared to withdraw if an internal revolution overthrew the democratic government.

A pragmatic foreign policy should take two factors into account: morals and the survival of the nation. Morals in foreign policy is a different concept from moralism. Morals has nothing to do with an ideological struggle; in fact, it is more of a restraining influence than anything else. A moral approach would make it impossible for the United States to interfere in the internal affairs of any nation—the Dominican Republic, Cuba, Vietnam—but would not prevent us from protecting a truly democratic nation from outside invasion. If and when we become mature enough to make exceptions to the policy of non-interference in a nation's internal affairs, it would be good to prove to the world that we still stand for the ideas we say we believe in by overthrowing the likes of Duvalier in Haiti, if interfere we must.

Faced with the prospect of world depression which would create more revolutions, coupled with our proven inability to police the world, we must change our outlook toward socialism and the legal nationalization of United States business abroad. We should trade with and aid those countries which make a serious attempt to conform with international law so that they won't be driven into alliances with belligerent countries. We lost Cuba's allegiance unnecessarily because of our basic antagonism toward her. By vowing to destroy her government, we forced her to turn to the only powerful nation able to offer the protection she needed. Had we supported her government—and it was a vast improvement over the previous regime—Cuba would no doubt be with us today. It might be possible, even now, to regain her confidence and allegiance through a sincere change of heart. The Castro government gave us every chance to be friends. But Cuba aside, we run the chance of emerging from the growing Vietnam quagmire with many more enemies than we now have if we employ our Cuban approach toward future socialist revolutions in the hungry world. Most of these countries will not be interested in our moralistic disputes: they will simply want to eat. We cannot impose reaction by force during a time when we ourselves may be having difficulty eating well. Perhaps the Enlightenment can be made to appeal to these newly emerging revolutionary governments—but only after they're fed. America wasn't a hungry nation in 1776. The Enlightenment cannot be forced upon nations by a nation that itself hasn't really practiced very much of the Enlightenment for fifty years.

If we are to understand what we have really been doing in Cuba and Vietnam, we should consider three points: (1) capitalism, (2) government control of business, and (3) the Big Red Scare. Capitalism, while allowed to run rampant in many respects in European countries during the eighteenth and much of the nineteenth century, ran completely uncontrolled in the heyday of imperialism in the countries that were weak enough for the European powers to be able to control their governments. The European governments themselves were not involved in foreign ventures as much as were the trading companies and private businessmen. While the necessity for more stringent controls on business and industry became obvious in the highly industrialized countries, these weaker nations remained pockets of cheap labor and economic anarchy as Europeans introduced social legislation at home. In Latin America, an area of particular concern to Americans, we continued to try to impose, by military force at times, conditions above which we ourselves had risen—all in the name of unrestrained profits. This continued through the Dulles era.

With the appearance of the Big Red Scare, the idealistic war against communism merged with the war against opposition to unrestrained business profits in underdeveloped countries. The Big Red Scare, in spite of the fear of bolshevism in other countries, was confined in its hysteria to America and Germany. After World War II, Britain replaced the stress on economic exploitation with a stress on economic improvement of colonies and underdeveloped nations. In the United States (if we can disregard our Cuban hysteria for a moment, or consider it a Dulles-era holdover) extreme government support for America's foreign business ventures melted away, at least temporarily, around 1960. Before the Big Red Scare, foreign-policy considerations were more practical. During the forty-year period from 1920 to 1960, practical considerations became mixed with holy considerations in varying degrees. Former minor economic goals became nearly worth unlimited war. By 1965 only the ideological holy war against communism remained as the primary consideration of American foreign policy. By now it did not matter if business was hurt. Business too must sacrifice to the threat all around us. Never mind the fact that sober analysts on Wall Street foresaw the dire consequences of Vietnam. They were too concerned with the profit motive, anyway—or so the government seemed to feel. If we were as selfish and practical and concerned with the fortunes of business in the nuclear age as in the nineteenth century, the Vietnam catastrophe might not have materialized at all. Capitalists suddenly found themselves with some of the same foreign-policy interests as socialists. None but the unsophisticated and those who actually believed in the domino theory could have supported that war. By all rights Wall Street should have been the scene of more anti-war demonstrations than any college campus. The historical interests of business in the earlier part of the twentieth century were not the same by the mid-1960's.

The security aspects of foreign affairs occasionally make it necessary for us to become involved in an issue regardless of apparent moral right and wrong if the nation's security is definitely threatened. The United States had no moral or security reason for the Bay of Pigs invasion, which, viewed in this light, was an indefensible act. On the other hand, even though Cuba may ostensibly have had the moral right to aim rockets at the United States, questions of security dictated that the rocket sites must be dismantled. Morals immediately become academic in such instances. There was no need to go further than to see that the threat to our security was removed, which was indeed as far as President Kennedy went before accepting compromise. We are not big or wealthy enough, even if it were within the spirit of Locke and Jefferson, to evangelistically expand the Enlightenment. Interference in Vietnam is immoral unless it can be defended as a matter of security to the United States, Australia, or other democracies. The really valid question is whether it is necessary. Any other reason rings of an evangelistic moralism that would have been perilous even in the pre-nuclear age. Such an approach by a thermonuclear armed superpower can easily be disastrous. The United States government must stop fooling the American people with empty issues and slogans. The very concept of democratic foreign policy demands that the nation be told the truth in order to arrive at an intelligent decision based on the security issues involved. Moralism has no place in the nuclear age.

But what of the real thermonuclear threat from China? First, of course, we must realize that our press has generally, with some notable exceptions again, bombarded us with a tremendous amount of one-sided propaganda in recent years with regard to China, as in Cuba and Vietnam. (There is a heartening trend toward responsibility in our national press. *Newsweek*, since changing ownership in recent years, *Time*, since the new editorial policy took shape in 1967, and the television networks have all shown increased responsibility of late.) On the other hand it is undeniable that China does persist in her unfortunate habit of cussing and swearing. If we assume that her leaders are rational, then we must take them at their word—that their avowed aim is to destroy our system and all we stand for. If we assume that they are not rational, then they could not be trusted with thermonuclear weapons in any event. All this has nothing to do with the Vietnam government or any other communistic government. Albania cusses and swears too, but she presents no threat. It would then seem, morals aside, that it is essential to the very life of the United States to destroy China's nuclear capability. This should not be construed as advocating conventional war against or conquest of China. It seems prudent, however, to take the Chinese government at its word, as we should have taken the Hitler government at its word, before it is too late. Destruction or dismantling of Chinese nuclear capabilities seems to be the likeliest solution. It would be necessary, of course, to elicit Soviet cooperation or at least tacit consent. This might involve some reciprocal guarantees on our part, such as demanding that France render herself nuclearly impotent, and a guarantee against West Germany's acquiring any nuclear decision-making power. The issue should be cemented by a solid non-proliferation pact. This would be similar to President Kennedy's action in the Cuban missile crisis. If bombing of Chinese nuclear installations became necessary, care would have to be taken not to war against the Chinese people—to keep our goals limited. It would not be a moral struggle, it would be a question of survival. We could then safely permit China to cuss and swear, as we do Albania. Not only would it be immoral to go any further than to guarantee our survival, but we have already shown that we are incapable of conquering even Vietnam, much less China. If we forced Chinese nuclear disarmament, we could lessen the blow at the same time with an offer of trade and access to our wheat surplus. (Past attempts to achieve a totalitarian state in European society have all fallen short of perfection. The term *totalitarianism* defines itself: total subjugation of the *total* or whole person to the state. A complete obliteration of independent thought in the twentieth-century European mind is of course impossible. In Mao's China, however, the story is much different. Here totalitarianism has been accepted by the masses with an enthusiasm only known before in Orwellian fantasies. Totalitarianism, a European invention, is much more adaptable to the Far East at this point in history.)

The Johnson administration represents the ultimate failure of "middle-aged, middle-class society." At the time of Kennedy's death it appeared to many that Johnson was incapable. But from the image of the typical loud-mouthed Texan bouncing about

Asia ostentatiously making an ass of himself, he immediately, upon taking office, began to act more in keeping with the dignity of the American presidency. He showed a sincere concern with domestic problems, from poverty to civil rights, but he continued to use stopgap measures that have characterized the federal government since the New Deal began. Progress could have been made had he not been committed to the Big Red Scare in foreign affairs. It was not Johnson's Great Society that bankrupted the nation, it was his abortive Vietnam War and his complete ignorance of money. The coming money crisis may carry with it the major advantage of ending that war. It should also end much of the American cockiness in foreign affairs and replace this with a pragmatic realization that our capabilities are limited. There could be no more horrible tragedy to crown the Vietnam War than if the United States, in a dying gasp of that dying leadership which has so far been broken only by Kennedy, were to drop the bomb in Vietnam instead of admitting her gross error. We would be forced to abandon the ruins if by chance the Soviets forewent direct retaliation. Such an act, if it did not end the world along with the old leadership, could well give the new leaders some of the same aura of past disgraces that the new generation of German leaders are compelled to face.

Today's liberals are making a sincere attempt, but they have not found the answer to our major problems. The answer does not seem to lie in the direction of more socialism. That has already failed us. Members of the New Left complain about such abstruse concepts as lack of identity, which, in old-fashioned terms, is loss of individuality. The conservatives have a point that big government *is* what diminishes individuality. Big government, as we have seen, is not generally compatible with "identity." It is truly the basis for totalitarianism. Big government seems to work in Scandinavia without any tinge of totalitarianism; but the Scandinavians are a very easygoing (and admirable) people, and their political units are small. The same is true of Britain and Switzerland. To arrive at a formula for our own nation, we must realize our unique problems. We must examine the mistakes of the New Deal and the cold war. We must take a sophisticated approach that can unemotionally examine the pros and cons of conservatism and liberalism. We need to take what is good from our heritage and discard that which is inimical to a twentieth-century extension of the Enlightenment. There is much to be valued and treasured in our past, not the least of which is our freedoms. The failure of the liberal idea of excessive spending for Vietnam may liberalize foreign policy. The liberals must admit soon that unlimited spending has failed, while those, both liberal and conservative, who were so cocky about foreign policy must admit the failure of United States Asian policy. Only by such humility on everyone's part can a sensible solution be reached.

FDR was truly the friend of the common man. But he was more of a sociologist than an economist. Rather than directly attack the problem of poverty, he concerned himself with half-hearted and halfway attempts to take care of symptoms. In his doing so, an inefficient bureaucracy was created that drained individuality from the citizen.

A concern with poverty should have been accepted at the time of the Industrial Revolution—if not at the time of the American Revolution—as the proper concern of government. Conservatives who denied this only hastened the counterrevolution and forced the liberals to enact a bureaucracy. Had conservatives offered a guaranteed annual wage after 1929, we might be in a much less uncomfortable predicament. But as Americans, and most of all as people, we are extremists. Reactionaries fight sensible as well as idiotic anti-poverty proposals. Socialists cry for bigger government and at the same time lament their loss of freedom. The time has come to bury our differences or face the consequences.

The depression of the thirties was erroneously blamed on the market crash. The market crash did not, of course, cause that depression. It was just the most graphic evidence that a serious mistake had been made. Unemployment became serious, not on the day after the market finished crashing but months afterward. If there were no organized market in securities, but all labor and real estate were handled in a handful of nationwide exchanges complete with charts and daily market averages, we would see a graphic picture of these markets deteriorating at an alarming pace and probably blame the loss in security values on the "labor market" or "real estate market" crash. Socialists who would do away with securities markets would only throw out a valuable, ready-made warning system in the highly refined statistics which accompany the money markets. There may have been some excuse for ignorance of the clear warning signals these presented in 1928–29; but there was no excuse in the Cold War Bull Market and the Vietnam Bear Market. The money markets are an alarm system that the government should use. If the government is so unknowing as to let the situation deteriorate enough to allow unwise money panics after periods of unwise growth rate, at least market statistics can show us what to expect in a few months so that we can prepare.

Conservatives, liberals, socialists, and communists alike are guilty of an undue stress on material things. This is characterized by greed over and above the elimination of poverty. The New Deal came about only after many formerly well-off people became temporarily out of funds rather than because of a concern for the truly and permanently underprivileged who are still with us today. The New Deal was *prosperity-oriented* rather than *poverty-oriented*. Prosperous communistic countries are noted for their philosophy of dialectical materialism. They mince no words in telling us what is important to them. Since World War I, materialism has become the policy of governments. Business depressions offer the opportunity for dictators to rise to power. National Socialism, the "most extreme manifestation of the twentieth century revolt against reason,"[3] offered something for everybody. For labor there was full employment; for business there were huge profits; for nationalists there was the expansion of Pan-Germanism; for racists there was official anti-Semitism. The Western democracies, especially the United States, have also revolted against reason. This is evident in our extremism, romanticism, inability to compromise, and materialism, and in the lack of appeal that the middle of the road—the path of moderation— has had in politics. The Pepsi-generation—the unlamented youth

---

[3] Pinson, *op. cit.*, p. 490.

cult which represents a dizzy refusal to learn and profit from the past—will die along with the cold-war prosperity. Conservatives have many excellent and vital viewpoints; so do liberals. It is our opportunity to put aside our selfish materialism and to profit and learn from all reasonable viewpoints.

There is a need for the New Left in both political parties—especially the Republican. There are serious elements of the counterrevolution in the doctrine of the Right and of the Left. The search for identity, or individuality, coupled with the elimination of poverty, lies in the moderate approach. At the moment this is represented principally by the moderate Republicans and some good Democrats. We have a New Left and a New Right. Let us have a group of New Moderates from both elements and dedicated to the preservation of American ideals. We have lambasted the New Left for its withdrawal from conventional politics and its refusal to seek power—not power as an end in itself but as an instrument for good. One restraint on the "arrogance of power" we might seek is a restraint on the power of the Commander in Chief in the nuclear age regarding the military in general and the bomb in particular. Such a measure would need be considered with great care in order not to hamper our retaliatory credibility. But as any statistician can easily confirm, the chance that the world can exist another hundred years on the condition that two nuclear-armed and dangerous nations who have, say, fifteen leaders each in a century will not accidentally get a power-mad nut at the head of one of the governments, is virtually nil. The goal of our generation is to avoid that probable nuclear war at all costs. To do so we must avoid past mistakes. And to do so will require determination:

> Every movement which exercises power by means of naked force is bound sooner or later to sacrifice whatever ideology it possesses to needs of maintaining itself in power. This was true of communism in the USSR and this was also true of Nazi ideology.[4]

One does not have to agree with my outlines for achieving economic goals in order to participate in this New Moderate move-

[4] Pinson, *op. cit.*, p. 488.

ment. The only requirement is the acceptance of reason and the philosophy of Burke—not his formula for what was needed for England in the late eighteenth century but his concept of change if needed, but only if needed. Above all the New Moderate position is not an apologetic or weak position. It seeks compromise where compromise is possible; it must refuse to compromise freedom. When Barry Goldwater, in his famous 1964 acceptance speech, which was the greatest speech on behalf of freedom since Patrick Henry's day, said, "Extremism in the defense of liberty is no vice. Moderation in the pursuit of justice is no virtue," he stated the very position that has been advocated throughout this book. The only difference is that the Senator did not know what he was talking about. And just as Marx said in one of his public appearances, "I am not a Marxist," so must the younger generation of the forties and fifties work toward keeping their ideas from being perverted. That, Mr. Holmes, is one thing left to declare.

ACKNOWLEDGMENTS

For arrangements made with various publishers whereby permission to reprint excerpts from copyrighted material has been granted, and for the courtesy extended by them and by their authors, the following acknowledgments are gratefully made:

Harper & Row, Publishers, Incorporated, for pages 45-46, 48-49, 56-60 from "The Big Red Scare" in *Only Yesterday* by Frederick Lewis Allen. Copyright 1931 by Frederick Lewis Allen; renewed, 1959, by Agnes Rogers Allen. Reprinted by permission of Harper & Row, Publishers.

D. C. Heath & Company, for excerpts from *The Age of Aristocracy, 1688-1830,* by William B. Willcox. Copyright 1966 by D. C. Heath & Company: Boston.

Alfred A. Knopf, Incorporated, for excerpts from *A History of the Modern World* by Robert R. Palmer with Joel Colton. Copyright 1950, 1956 by Alfred A. Knopf, Inc. Reprinted by permission of the publisher, Alfred A. Knopf, Inc.

The Macmillan Company, a subsidiary of Crowell Collier and Macmillan, Incorporated, for excerpts from *Modern Germany* by Koppel S. Pinson. Reprinted by permission of the publishers, The Macmillan Company.

Newsweek, Incorporated, for the article "Burned Up" which appeared on page 29 of the July 3, 1967, issue of *Newsweek.* Copyright, Newsweek, Inc., July, 1967.

Charles Scribner's Sons, for excerpts from *The Mind of Germany* by Hans Kohn. Reprinted by permission of Charles Scribner's Sons.

The University of Chicago Press, for excerpt from *American Diplomacy 1900–1950* by George F. Kennan. Copyright 1951 by the University of Chicago.

Index of Persons